Alfred Austin

England's Darling

Alfred Austin

England's Darling

ISBN/EAN: 9783744708890

Printed in Europe, USA, Canada, Australia, Japan

Cover: Foto ©ninafisch / pixelio.de

More available books at **www.hansebooks.com**

ENGLAND'S DARLING

ENGLAND'S DARLING

BY

ALFRED AUSTIN

POET LAUREATE

A.D. 878. This year the Danish Army rode over the land of the West Saxons, where they settled, and drove many of the people over the sea; and, of the rest, the greatest part they rode down, and subdued to their will. ALL BUT ALFRED THE KING.
Anglo-Saxon Chronicle.

Génie composite, à la fois pratique et passionné, Alfred fut un vrai Anglais.   JUSSERAND.

London
MACMILLAN AND CO.
AND NEW YORK
1896

All rights reserved

TO

HER ROYAL HIGHNESS

ALEXANDRA, PRINCESS OF WALES

DAUGHTER OF VANISHED VIKINGS

AND

MOTHER OF ENGLISH KINGS TO BE

I RESPECTFULLY TENDER

THIS INADEQUATE RECORD

OF

THE GREATEST OF ENGLISHMEN

PREFACE

In the spacious gallery of commanding characters commemorated in English Poetry, there is a strange and unaccountable blank. Where we look for the most illustrious figure of all, there is an empty niche. The greatest of Englishmen has never been celebrated by an English poet. Though it still be true of our race, as of those concerning whom Tacitus wrote, "Celebrant carminibus antiquis quod unum apud illos memoriæ et annalium genus est," no Englishman has sung of Alfred the Great. Extolled by a succession of prose historians, by Asser, by Ethelwerd, by Florence of Worcester, by William of Malmesbury, and deeply rooted in the affections of his countrymen by an unbroken tradition, which, for a thousand years, has designated him "England's Darling," Alfred is forgotten by Chaucer, all but ignored by Spenser, unnamed by Shakespeare, and but fortuitously alluded to by the most eminent of their successors. Shakespeare indeed, though bequeathing us in *Lear* and *Cymbeline* two Celtic dramas, has no Saxon hero, no Saxon theme. Tributes to the genius, the virtue, the fortitude, of Alfred abound in the prose writings, not of Englishmen alone, but of annalists and moralists writing in foreign tongues. "Ille inter fremitus armorum et stridores lituorum leges tulit," says William of Malmesbury in a sentence of singular strength, in which the glory of battle and the dignity of jurisprudence are harmoniously associated. In his *Outlines of the History of the World*, one of his earlier researches which are insufficiently known to the present generation, Gibbon thus expresses himself concerning Alfred: "Amidst the deepest gloom of barbarism, the virtue of Antoninus, the learning and valour of Cæsar, and the legislative genius of Lycurgus, shine forth united in that patriot King. Several of his institutions have survived the Norman Conquest, and contributed to form the English Constitution." Hume, little given to enthusiasm, and never betrayed into exaggeration, asserts that "this Prince, by his great virtues and shining talents, saved his country from utter ruin and subversion." Burke concludes a stately panegyric with this compendious verdict: "In a word, Alfred comprehended, in the greatness of his mind, the whole of government and all its parts at once; and, what is most difficult to human frailty, was at the same time sublime and minute." Voltaire, to whose mocking wit not even the maiden deliverer of his own country was sacred, mingles no sneer with his homage to Alfred. "Je ne sais," he writes, "s'il y a jamais eu sur la terre un homme plus digne des respects de la posterité qu'Alfred le Grand." Mirabeau draws a parallel between Alfred and Charlemagne, and assigns the palm for greatness to the former. Herder, in his outlines of *A Philosophy of a History of Man*, pronounces a similar verdict. "A pattern for Kings in times of extremity, a bright star in the history of mankind, living a century after Charlemagne, he was perhaps a greater man in a circle more limited." Shakespeare affirms

> . . . We are not ourselves
> When nature, being oppressed, commands the mind
> To suffer with the body.

But Alfred rose as superior to fleshly ailment as to the inertness of his subjects and the ferocity of his foes. Later historians have but repeated the conclusion of their predecessors; nor has searching modern scholarship removed from Alfred's brow a single leaf of the fivefold laurel of King, Soldier, Poet, Lawgiver, and Saint, that has for ten hundred years encircled it.

Strange therefore is it that Alfred hitherto has been glorified in no English poem. But the omission seems stranger still when we observe that, by his birth, his character, and his exploits, he is the one Englishman pre-eminently fitted to be a National Hero. The person elevated by instinctive selection to that commanding position must have existed, yet should loom, in outlines imposingly vague, through the mist of receding centuries. He must be, at one and the same time, historical and mythical. Arthur is too exclusively the one. The greatest of our Edwards and our Harrys are too clearly the other. Who will warrant the existence of Arthur more than of Brute or of Merlin? The Flos Regum of Bardic story has not flesh-and-blood enough to enforce full homage from our imagination. Moreover, Arthur is a Celtic, not a Saxon Prince; and the tactful genius of an exquisite poet has abstained from enduing him with more than a limited number of somewhat negative virtues. Cressy, Poitiers, and Agincourt, are names never to be forgotten. But more than one reproach adheres to the memory of Edward the Third, the sunset of his brilliant Reign having been darkened, not only by public misfortune, but by the malign influence of a grasping mistress and unpopular favourites; while Shakespeare has stamped on our minds an ineradicable recollection of the youthful levities of Henry the Fifth. But Alfred has neither stigma nor stain. A ruler without arrogance, a soldier without personal ambition, a lawgiver devoid of pedantry, a poet free from vanity, a saint untainted by fanaticism, Alfred laid the foundation, in days of distracting trouble, of our society, our language, and our naval power. The records of him may be scanty, but they suffice; and he towers before us, actual if indefinite. While he is placed, thanks to the historian, on a solid and visible pedestal, around his head shimmers the magnifying halo of tradition. By affectionate fable he is apotheosised above ordinary humanity. But the qualities that at times seem distantly divine, leave him still invested with the familiar and winning attributes of man.

But if Alfred be thus qualified, alike by our knowledge and by our ignorance, to figure as the Hero of a Nation, his credentials become still more conclusive, when we note what is the nation he typifies and represents. Englishmen have never conceded unqualified admiration save to those who combined with intellectual distinction the crowning grace of moral worth. A Louis the Eleventh, a Henri Quatre, a Louis the Fourteenth, a Voltaire, a Rousseau, a Mirabeau, would never have secured the unreserved homage of English sentiment. We forgive much to patriotism, we condone much in genius; but we accept no one as absolute monarch of our affections whose record is not clean. Our Ideal, it must be owned, is lofty and exacting; for we claim for our Hero a combination of qualities that blend with difficulty, and which in common estimate are deemed almost contradictory. Yet we find them in Alfred; it may be added, in Alfred alone. An obedient son to a father of unstable judgment and faltering virtue; a deferential brother to a Prince glaringly his inferior; a Ruler masculinely just yet femininely tender, Alfred moved between the realm of thought and the domain of action with alert but infallible footsteps; ordering his days and distributing his faculties with discriminating concern between the harmonious development of his own nature and the immediate rescue of the State. He cherished the companionship of scholars, but was never subjected to their sway; and his thoughtful devotion to the Church was wisely tempered by a steadfast vindication of what is due to Cæsar. He had the very talents, and the very character, that Englishmen admire: an imagination at once speculative and practical, with feet firmly planted on the earth, yet with forehead questioning the sky; a virile love of country, an unwearied appetite for work, innate reverence for law, attachment to family and home, a grave responsiveness to duty, high-bred modesty, the determination not to be overcome, and an utter absence of pretension. Well may Englishmen revere these qualities in Alfred; for, while they constitute him their ideal and their darling, they are the qualities which founded, and which can alone maintain, the English Empire.

For himself, the author cannot remember the time when Alfred was not the hero of his affections. Alfred's name, and the tales that clustered round it, formed the most enthralling pages of nursery erudition; and the fond partiality of childhood was sanctioned by study, and confirmed by life. Wantage and

Athelney became sacred names. When first he stood in the Roman Forum, where the buffaloes then took their noonday siesta in the recumbent shafts of Sabine wine-carts, he used to wonder how it looked when Alfred, sent to the Eternal City by his father "with an honourable escort," was anointed future King, and adopted as spiritual son, by Leo the Fourth; and he remembered how, when Alfred had justified Leo's spiritual insight, Pope Martin, out of regard for the King's great deeds and spotless character, freed the school of the Anglo-Saxons in Rome from all tax and tribute. Over and over again, in later years, when traversing those tracts of our native land which the most vividly recall his heroism, his wisdom, and his triumph, I found myself exclaiming, "If one could but write of Alfred!" A visit to Edington—the Saxon Ethandune—one mellow November afternoon, gave fresh stimulus to the longing, and finally generated the production of this work. Would it were worthier! But, to cite words of Alfred's own, "Do not blame me; for every man must say what he says, and do what he does, according to his ability."

Meagre, comparatively, as are the memorials,

PREFACE

whether authentic or disputable, of the second half of the ninth century respecting our Island, they are not so scanty as is commonly affirmed. I was astonished, in my search for any scrap of fact or fable that by suggestiveness might aid my purpose, to find the materials so ample. For every incident in the following poem there is a foundation, however slight, in written record or in oral hearsay, not only concerning Alfred himself, but equally as regards his brilliant son. Alfred reigned for three-and-twenty winters after the victory of Ethandune and Chippenham; but, since the close of his days was, happily, not tragic, the action of the poem ceases at a moment dramatically more conclusive. It was only by Will that Alfred bequeathed to his wife the Manors of Wantage and Athelney, and by the same instrument that he manumitted his serfs.[1] But I have not hesitated to antedate those and other incidents of his Rule, and, in a word, to compress into a period of a

---

[1] What a delight it would have been to the studious King, could he have read, in a fragment of Hellanicus, how the slaves that had fought on the Athenian side at Arginusæ were manumitted, and enrolled among the Platæans. Τοὺς συνναυμαχήσαντας δούλους Ἑλλάνικός φησιν ἐλευθερωθῆναι, καὶ ἐγγραφέντας ὡς Πλαταιεῖς συμπολιτεύεσθαι αὐτοῖς.

few weeks the most striking events of a lifetime. It is an interesting, and surely an auspicious, coincidence that the present Heir to the English Throne, like the Atheling in Alfred's Reign, bears the name of Edward, and again, like his mighty namesake, has for Consort a lovely Dane.

"Alfred, Edward, and such proper names," says the learned Wright, "have become part of our language. There can be no doubt that Anglo-Saxons would have written them Ælfred, Eadweard; but there is no more reason for our printing them so in a modern English book, than there would be for our printing *æfter* for *after*, or *eall* for *all*." So also it seems to me; and, if use is here made of the Saxon "Ealdorman," it is because the modern form of that word would have suggested misleading associations.

The English language, as it now exists, is indebted for its volume and variety to many tributaries; and we owe it to our mother-tongue not to allow it to be impoverished by gratuitous prejudice against any one of its sources. The attempt to exalt the Saxon over the Latin elements of our language can never be more than an exhibition of philological pedantry. But one perforce felt that, in portraying a period anterior to the days when the Latin and Romance literatures gradually enriched the vocabulary of Beowulf, one was bound to eschew, as far as might be, glaring anachronisms of speech. Hence, save occasionally in the mouth of Alfred himself, and of the scholarly ecclesiastics he summoned to his side, the language used by the characters in *England's Darling* is mainly if not exclusively Saxon in its origin—the natural utterance of English men and women living in the ninth century of our Era.

A thousand years ago! If one turns to the Saxon Chronicle, one may read, at that date: "Then King Alfred gave orders for building long ships against the esks, which were full nigh twice as long as the others. Some had sixty oars, some more, and they were both swifter and steadier, and also higher than the others." The Chronicle goes on to tell how the King commanded his men to go out against the enemy with nine of the new ships, and prevent escape to the outer sea; and how they took two of the Danish esks, drove others ashore, and crippled the rest. Thus Swanage was the precursor of Trafalgar. A thousand years ago! What a splendid, what an animating anniversary! And should the genius of

Alfred continue to inspire his race, why should we hesitate to believe that, a thousand years forward from to-day, his name will still be honoured, and the Sceptre he saved be still upheld, by a romantic, resolute, and invincible People?

A. A.

PERSONAGES

ALFRED	*Surnamed the Great.*
EDWARD	*His Son.*
PLEGMUND	*Archbishop of Canterbury.*
WEREFRITH	*Bishop of Worcester.*
ETHELRED	*Alfred's Son-in-law (afterwards Ealdorman of Mercia).*
ETHELNOTH	*Ealdorman of Somerset.*
ETHELSWITHA	*Alfred's Wife.*
ETHELFRIDA	*His Daughter (married to Ethelred).*
EDGIVA	*A Danish Maiden.*

THANES, EALDORMEN, FREEMEN, SERFS, ETC.

PLACE.

Athelney—Selwood—Ethandune.

TIME—A.D. 878.

ACT I

SCENE I

[The Saxon Fastness in Athelney.]

PLEGMUND.

Know you the tidings?

ETHELNOTH.

          No, nor crave to hear,
In these ill days.

WEREFRITH.

          Withal, to know the worst
Is the one way whereby to better it.

ETHELNOTH.

Out with it then!

PLEGMUND.

     Buhred hath fled the land
By him for two-and-twenty winters swayed,
Fled oversea, a runaway to Rome,
And in the seat of Mercia Ceowulf rules.
Rules, did I say? Nay, grovels at the nod
Of Guthrum who, forsworn, upholds him there,
A Saxon thane, withal a Danish serf,
Where Alfred's sister sate below her lord,
Helping him rule.

ETHELRED.

And she?

WEREWULF.

     Held fast the ground,
With a firm few, against the heathen horde,
Egbert's true grandchild, long as living force
Could break the onset, but at length withdrew,
And, backward-wending pilgrims say, was seen
Treading the streets of Pavia all alone,
Seeking her lord.

WEREFRITH.

    From far Northumbria
Blow news as luckless. Breaking up his camp,
That by the Tyne had wintered, Halfdene bursts
Over the land, and, ravaging it, rides
Right to the march and border of the Picts.
Among his thanes he parcels out the soil,
And the long-haired Northumbrian freemen makes
Harrowers and ploughers to their conquerors,
Clipped to the nape.

PLEGMUND.

      Aye, and fouler still,
Hingvar and Hubba, since King Edmund slain,
Lashed to a trunk and arrow-shot to death,
Ride through East Anglia rifling shrine and cell,
Ely and Croyland, Bardeney, Peterborough,
Breaking and burning, and at very Mass
Wrenching the chalice from the hand of God,
And tearing from the abbot's tonsured brow
Alb, stole, and chasuble. Nor this the worst,
Where worse awaits. From virgins vowed to Heaven,
Virgins as white as is the Yuletide snow,

They strip the veil; who straightway die of shame,
Or, dreader doom, dwell penned within the sty
Of wallowing sea-swine.

ETHELRED.

                The outlandish dogs,
Uprooting Egbert's England, and afresh
Untwisting what he bound, and to their will
Enserfing all.

ETHELNOTH.

              Nay, Ethelred, not all!
ALL BUT ALFRED THE KING!

ETHELRED.

Pray Heaven he lives! But, while he roams abroad,
Now in this cloak, now that, swordless, alone,
Spying the where and whither of his foes,
I still must lie with fear for bedfellow.

PLEGMUND.

Nay, sign the cross upon your brow and sleep.
Since by Pope Leo he was hallowed King,
Heaven keeps a watch upon his chosen head.

ETHELRED.

May you rede rightly, Plegmund! And belike
Is mother-wit a sort of Providence,
Whereof is Alfred's brain as stocked as though
It nothing housed beside; for commonly—
Forgive me, good Archbishop!—learning blunts
The native shrewdness of the mind. In him
Are layman sense and cleric wisdom twin;
And though his brain is swayed by thought, his hand
Keeps just as steady on the hilt as though
He knew no more than I or Ethelnoth.

PLEGMUND.

God bless your simpleness! So long as men
Know how like you to strike for Mother-land,
By the rood! they are wise enough.

ETHELNOTH.

      O true Archbishop!
May England never lack anointed lips,
Like these, to preach Christ's gospel manfully!

SCENE II

[A clearing in the forest. EDWARD, sitting on some faggot-wood, is stringing together bluebells and primroses which he has just gathered. A misselthrush is singing overhead.]

EDWARD.

Sing, throstle, sing,
   On the hornbeam bough;
But tell not the King
   Of a maiden's vow.
When the heart is ripe,
   Then the days are fleet:
Pipe, throstle, pipe!
   Sweet! sweet! sweet!

If but the best of us could sing like thee!
But even Adhelm lacks the craft to reach
Thy untaught silvery syllables of song,
Wild gleeman of the woods! In all the world
There lives no sound to match thy minstrelsy,
Saving her voice; and that, though heavenlier still,
Alack! is seldom heard.

> *Flute, throstle, flute,*
>   *To my lagging dear,*
> *And never be mute*
>   *Till she hie to hear.*
> *Now that the Spring*
>   *And the Summer meet,*
> *Sing, throstle, sing!*
>   *Sweet! sweet! sweet!*

[He hears a rustling in the leaves, and bounds to his feet.]

She comes! But no, it is a tattered churl,
That through the tangle of these troubled times
Seeks for an outlet to his wretchedness.
Yet, better not be seen: Love's hide-and-seek
Wants no onlookers.

[He swings himself on to a bough, and swarms the tree. ALFRED, disguised as a vagrant, passes underneath, pausing an instant, and taking up the flowers that are lying on the ground.]

ALFRED.

Children, or lovers, must have passed this way,
Or lovers therefore children; for the twain
Have this in common, that they lightly cull

The sweets of nature, but to throw away
And let them wilt when gathered.

[*He lays the flowers on the ground and passes on.*]

EDWARD.

He mutters to himself some droneful saw,
After his kind.   The very primroses
To his sad gaze beseem but ruefully;
And little kens he that those bluebells keep,
There where they lie, within their threaded stems,
The secret of a joy unspeakable.
But lo! a nest, and five blue eggs still warm
With love's close brooding!   If the misselthrush
That shrilled so gleefully till scared away
Had mated here, I must have spared his crib.
But never doth he build as high as this.
True poet that he is, he nesteth low,
Only to soar in song!   These eggs bespeak
The satin-shining starling, whistling thief,
Who mocks his betters and parades aloft
On borrowed notes.   So will I filch these beads,
To make my woodland wreath still worthier
For her white throat.

[He descends the tree, blows the eggs, and threads them with the primroses and bluebells. Holding them out before him]

A necklace for a queen.

EDGIVA (*coming noiselessly from behind the faggot-stack, and kneeling in front of him*).

      The queen is here!
For love can seat the lowliest on a throne,
And—do you love me?

EDWARD (*raising her*).

      Sceptre is there none,
Sceptre nor sword, should these be mine to give,
I would not halve with you.

EDGIVA.

      Halve but yourself,
And 'twere enough. Nay, give it all to me,
And never take away! But will you not,
For true love's sake, entrust to me your name,
That I may say it when you are not near,
And, saying it, may fancy you less far?

EDWARD.

Know me as Edward; 'tis a princely name:
And if the world should ever call me prince,
Be sure that you my princess then would be.

EDGIVA.

Noble you *must* be: noble too am I,
If true the tale that Danewulf loves to tell
When twilight duskens round the crackling logs;
How, striding hearthward through the forest glade,
He heard a mewling in an eagle's nest,
And, swarming to the wychelm's topmost fork,
Found me, strange callow nestling, not yet fledged,
A golden fillet round my dimpled wrist,
Awake and wailing; cradled there, he deems,
By widowed chieftain worsened in the fight,
And fleeing for his life.

EDWARD.

                    No! dropped from Heaven.
Too fair, too sweet, for any seed of earth,
My blossom of the air, my sky-sent gift,

My love from otherwhere, with not a touch
Of the gross ground!

EDGIVA.

O woodland way of love!
Wealthiest of all, that never says enough
Till every flower be hired by lordly speech
To bear its burden.

EDWARD.

More, much more, than speech!
Look! I have made a necklace for your neck,
Worthy its fresh and fair simplicity.
The Pagans have our gold and jewels filched,
And left us nought but steel, wherewith, please Heaven!
We'll have the gold and jewels back again:
So for your throat I have neither ore nor gem.
Yet gaze hereon! These golden primroses,
These topaz shells, these bells of amethyst,
Are—nay, but let me round them on your neck,
And then with kisses pay your jewel-smith.

[*He fastens them round her throat.*]

EDGIVA.

How you all spoil me! You, the most of all!
My mother,—other mother have I none,
And she no other child,—Danewulf's free wife,
Is fain to hinder me when I would drudge,
Vowing that hand of woman noble-born
Should touch nought baser than the dainty task
Of pirn or needle; but I heed her not:
And these poor arms you fold about you now,
Oft scrub the settle, scour the pans, and knead
The homely dough. You handle but the sword!

[Breaking away from him.]

I am not meet for you.

EDWARD (*embracing her tenderly*).

So much more meet,
Because you are a woman, scorning not
A woman's duty. For my father says,
Work is the noblest lot and life of man,
While war is but the weapon wrought to clear
A path for peaceful labour.

EDGIVA.

     I should love
To know your father.

EDWARD.

    So you shall, some day,
When, Alfred's peaceful daydreams all fulfilled,
Men may beneath their roof-tree safely sit,
Not harried by these rovers of the sea,
This way, and that, finding no settled home
For such a winsome tenderling as thou!

EDGIVA.

Last night I had a dream, a foolish dream,—
Nay, shall I tell it you? for still you count
My folly wisdom,—an unmeaning dream,
Withal that haunts me waking,—how there shone
Out of my body in the ebon night
A light—a light!—that, steady as a star,
But dazzling as the noonday sun in heaven,
Lighted all England!

EDWARD (*folding his arms round her*).

                Dream that may come true,
My fair soothsayer! But till then, no word
Of this . . . the highest, heavenliest thing on earth!

EDGIVA.

Now come and see my home. The needfire burns
With no more tell-tale watch than one old serf,
That craved for passing bit and sup within,
And whom my mother set beside the hearth
To heed the griddle-cakes, the while she sped
To milk the wayward goats; and Danewulf too
Is far amid the clearing, raking mast,
To fat the hogs. Come! just a little while.

SCENE III

[The interior of DANEWULF'S Hut. ALFRED is sitting before the hearth, scanning a map of England, sketched by himself.]

ALFRED.

Yes, thus I trace it, ocean-fashioned land,

And wrinkled by the waves, that, rolling round
Its rough irregular shore, run out and in,
Following it always as though loth to leave,
Nay eager, were they let, to find a way
To its very heart! England! Once Egbert's England,
And his to be again, if Heaven but deign
Use my poor brain and blade to wrench it back
For Christ and Cerdic's race! Northumbria,
Cradle and cloister of the learnëd Bede,
My ne'er seen master! Rude East-Anglia,
Shouldering the ocean, as to push them off
Who dare to come too close: Twice sacred Kent,
Whither came Cæsar first, Augustine next,
To win the isle to Government and God!
Then my own Wessex woods and fastnesses,
Creeks, bays, bluffs, combes, and shoreward-setting
    streams,
Crowned at their source with burgh and sanctuary
Now menaced by the Dane, and fenced in north
By Buhred's Mercia, Buhred overcome,
And feebly flying where he should have stood,
And won, or died. For all of these were Egbert's.
Aye, and the western shire's once glorious lord,
Adhelm's Geraint, owned Egbert Overlord,

Even to the uttermost point of land where sounds
Nought save the billows shocking herbless crags,
Or seagulls wheeling over wind-lashed waves.
Aye and beyond, where on from Wye to Dee
Runs Offa's Dyke, and Celt with Saxon live
In kindred husbandry,—Grant me, God King!
I Alfred, your weak servant, yet may be
Law to North Wales and terror to Strathclyde,
And thus this side the mist may shape, within,
One England, outward sheltered by the surge
Against the spoiler!

    [He folds the map, and takes out his hornbook.]

                         But enough of hope,
Never made good save seconded by deed,
And deed's forerunner, thought. I broke off here,
So here I must run on; that those who come
After my going may have means to learn
How fared it with their forebears, like to me,
Who strove with lack of learning, spelling out
The time-smudged tales and charters of the Past,
Unto them adding truthful chronicle
Of our own deeds in this our mother-tongue,
Best bond of kinship, that shall weld in one
Jute, Angle, Frisian, aye and these fierce Danes,

Not alien to our cradle, once enforced
To own the lordship of the Saxon sword.

[He resumes the writing of the Chronicle. Meanwhile, EDWARD and EDGIVA have approached the Hut, and are about to enter.]

EDGIVA.

Hist! Mother is within: I hear her voice.
Bide here awhile; I will be back anon.
Quit me not yet! Love still hath more to say.

[EDWARD remains without. EDGIVA, entering, finds her mother upbraiding ALFRED for allowing the cakes to scorch.]

EDGIVA.

Nay, mother, but you must not flout him thus.
Heed his gray hairs, look on his furrowed brow,
And that strange something which nor you, nor I,
Nor any of the level breed of folk,
Have in their seeming. 'Tis a scholar's face,
With far-off gaze, away in other lands,
Whither we may not fare nor follow him.
Look on his inkhorn. Nay, be quieted:
I'll rasp the cakes; they're but a trifle singed,
And we shall sup in plenty.

[DANEWULF's wife, still muttering her laments, leaves ALFRED and EDGIVA alone.]

EDGIVA.

                      Heed her not.
She is a faithful housewife, and her thought
Ran on the loaves so keenly, that you feel
The sharpness of its edge.

ALFRED.

                      And rightfully
She rates my fault. I should have watched the hearth,
Nor failed in the plain task she set me to,
The price of shelter.

EDGIVA.

                      Who would heed such things,
With a great book before him?

ALFRED.

                      But he should,
My kindly maid, if such his hiring be;
And I am sore to blame. Life's needful work
Should be done best by him that reads and writes,
Not absently forgone; for 'tis no gain

To be in letters wiser than your kind,
Withal in life more witless.

EDGIVA.

      Would that I
Could read and write!

ALFRED.

      Then so you shall, some day,
And I will be your teacher.
  [He observes the golden bracelet on her arm.]
       Where, forsooth,
Gat you this armlet?

EDGIVA.

      Where myself was got,
In the green cradle of a rocking elm:
Left by a flying father, so 'tis guessed,—
But 'tis a longsome story. Say me when
You'll come and make me bookish, like yourself;
And then together will we watch the cakes,
Nor let them scorch.

ALFRED.

To-morrow am I bound
To the King's Witan, held in Athelney,
Now the May moon is rounding to the full.
And haply many a sevennight will pass
Ere that again my footsteps tend your way.
But see!

[*He takes out of the folds of his peasant's smock a polished oval crystal, inlaid with mosaic enamel, green and yellow, representing the outline of a human figure, which is seated, and holds in each hand a lilystalk. On the back of the crystal is a thin plate of gold, on which a flower is indicated. The oval-shaped side of the crystal is surrounded by a setting of gold filigree-work, on which are engraved the words,* AELFRED MEC HEHT GEWYRCAN.]

Take this, my pledge of thankfulness
For service timely paid. Show it to none,
Until, if ever, to the fastnesses
Where Alfred holds his camp, you chance to fare;
Then with it ask of any, they will find
And lead you to the scholar who for now
Prays you Godspeed.

EDGIVA.

Every bright star in Heaven
Shine on your going!

[ALFRED quits the Hut, and goes his way. EDGIVA comes out to look for EDWARD, but cannot find him.]

EDGIVA.

O, he has gone, albeit I begged him stay,
And no word said when come he will again,
Leaving me reckon the time without the hope
That makes it shorter.

EDWARD (*from his hiding-place*).

Follow, if you can!

[He runs into the forest, EDGIVA following, and is recognised by ALFRED as he does so.]

ALFRED (*to himself*).

Edward! . . . Unkingly boy! In these stern times
To fleet the May thus softly! But, in youth,
As in these springtime saplings of the glade,
Floweth the mead of heedless wantonness,
That will not take life gravely! And the maid?
Sooth, he hath chosen well,—if honestly;
And she, being honest, needs will keep him so,—
Since 'tis the woman that keeps clean the man,—
Till I make inquest of his purposes.

[He passes on.]

EDGIVA.

Stop! stop! I can no more; you are too fleet
For feeble feet to follow!

[*She sinks on the ground, and* EDWARD *goes back to her.*]

EDWARD.

     Out of breath!
So, weaker for my wooing! Woo me back!
Not even strength for that, my panting prize,
Whom I have caught since me she could not catch,
So keep within my toils! Buy off the spear,
Or bear it, says the saw.

EDGIVA.

     There! there! enough!
You would outdo the doves upon the bough,
And, save you cease, there will be nothing, soon,
To hold a captive.

EDWARD.

     Pay lip ransom then,
And so be free, until enslaved again—
Again—again—and ever yet again!

EDGIVA.

Be seemly in your sweetness. Should he turn,
Who dwindles in the distance, he would spy
Your madcap ways, and——

EDWARD.

What! the muttering hind?
What should he reck of Mayday merriment,
That hinders not his going?

EDGIVA.

He a hind!
'Tis a skilled clerk, who reads—and writes—and gave
This crystal to my care. . . . Oh! I forgot!
Show it to none, he said. But you, you are
Only myself—my——

EDWARD.

Well, then show it me.

[She shows him the crystal.]

EDWARD.

The King's!

EDGIVA.

What said you, dear? I did not understand.

EDWARD.

That 'tis a crystal of no common worth.
What said he with the gift?

EDGIVA.

      Gift it was not,
Only a token-pledge to make me free
Of Alfred's Camp at Athelney, whene'er
I seek the scholar whom I strove to snatch
From mother's rating when the cakes got singed,
Whileas he bowed intent upon his book,
Instead of heeding them.
    [Seeing him still pensive.]
      What is it, Edward?

EDWARD.

Nothing, dear maid, save wonder at the wealth
Entrusted to your keeping.

EDGIVA.

      Do you fear
The gem is stolen? I can catch him up,
And give it back to him.

EDWARD.

                No : better bide ;
Choosing a timelier hour to test its spell,
And his who gave it you.

EDGIVA.

               He promised me
That I should learn to read ; and——

EDWARD.

                      Nay, forbear !
Nor with sour learning curdle your sweet soul,
Now all as fresh as newly-uddered milk.
Unlettered love is lore enough for you,
And eke for me.

EDGIVA.

             But you can read and write ;
And, did I read, you then could write to me,
And, did I write, you then of me could read,
Some trusty bearer running twixt us twain,
And keeping us together all the while,
No longer held apart for days on days,

Days—weeks—O, should it stretch into a month,
I could not bear it.

EDWARD.

            Yet, forsooth, it may!
Now listen, and be staid! I love you, sweet!
But, when the sword is out, why then farewell
To fondlings of the forest; and the time
Is big with blows of blade and battle-axe;
And, should the looked-for shock be on us soon,
I must be there!

EDGIVA.

          Then so indeed must I.

EDWARD.

That, you must not; nor yet to Athelney
Hie, ere I bring, or send, you greeting word.
For, as I trust my sword, do you trust me,
And know that, should it strike as straight and true
As is my purpose, I will bring it back,
Shut in its sheath, and lay it at your feet.

EDGIVA.

When will that be?

EDWARD.

No man can tell his weird.
God knows, Who sits above us, and to Him
I you entrust. So be nor sad nor lone.

EDGIVA.

I never can be lonely nor yet sad
With such a love as yours to hearten me.
Only, I pray you, do not die, nor leave
Me utterly without you. While you live,
I can bear all things.

EDWARD.

Spoken as I wished.

EDGIVA.

I have no wish except to do your wish;
For man is masterful, and so should be,
And I am but a woman; having strength
To hide my weakness, thus to keep you strong,
But feeble all beside. You love me, don't you?

EDWARD.

This morning when I rose to wend your way,
'Twas barely dawn, and herding night had not
Yet folded all her stars.   But, as I clove
Straight through the low-lying marsh, then leaped to
    land,
Tethering my boat among the reedy swamps
Where fish the flapping herons, soon the East
Crimsoned like hedgerose yet but half unclosed,
Then opened, and the day waxed frank and fresh
As she towards whom with hither-hastening feet
I fared, I flew.   The treble-throated lark
Shook his wet wings, and, soon an unseen sound,
Carolled his matin at the gate of Heaven.
But whether like a fountain he went up,
Or in melodious spray fell bubbling back,
Upward or downward, still he seemed to trill
"Edgiva" and "Edgiva," till your name
Soared into space, and summered all the air.
Why do you weep?

EDGIVA.

                There is no tongue save tears
To say how happy your fond madness makes me.

EDWARD.

Then, as I crossed the Parrett where it swirls
Swelled by the Ile and Yeo, a mottled trout,
That motionless beneath an alder kept
Its poise against the current, sudden scared,
Flashed like a flying shadow through the stream,
And was no more; and like to it I sped,
Swift up the windings of the wave that points
The pathway to your home.   The ladysmocks
Smiled on me as I passed, "She waits! she waits!"
And every wilding windflower that I bruised
Seemed to upbraid the slowness of my feet.
And so I was too soon,—love always is,—
And made a pastime of this flowery chain
To link you to me still when I am gone.
Look! when it fades, frame you another like it,
And then another, that the woven bond
Betwixt us twain may never be undone.

EDGIVA.

Nay, when this wilteth, I will wear it still,
Not round my neck, but nearer, next my heart,
Until you come again.

EDWARD.

               Then, now farewell!
See! Kiss my sword, and pray upon your knees
Nightly, and with each quivering of the dawn,
That it may strike as true as is my troth,
For God and England!

END OF ACT I

ACT II

SCENE I

[Athelney. Serfs are carrying loads to a barn near the King's Camp.]

FIRST SERF.

Fetch me a hunk of salted flitch,
 And a jug of sweetened ale,
And off I trudge to bank the ditch,
 Or bang about the flail.
Who recks of summer sweat and swink,
 Or winter's icy pang?
Tilt up the mug, my mates, and drink,
 And let the world go hang,
   Go hang,
And let the world go hang.

SECOND SERF.

Now, youngsters, snap the fallen sticks,
  Now, hearthwife, boil the pot,
For we have thatched the barley ricks,
  And ploughed the gafol plot.
The shepherd's star begins to wink,
  The she-wolf whets her fang;
Up with the mead-bowl, mates, and drink,
  And let the world go hang,
    Go hang,
  And let the world go hang!

THIRD SERF.

'Tis but a lean life we lead in Athelney. More tuns of marsh water, I warrant, than combs of smooth ale.

FIRST SERF.

Aye, and with sopping sedge to lie on, o'nights. But, after bearing planks to make ready the Witan for the King and the King's thanes, one 'ud sleep on a midden heap, were it dead froze. But that's done with; and now to stack all this gear afore noon.

[Alfred, still disguised as a peasant, passes by.]

SECOND SERF (*to Alfred*).

Lend us a hand, gaffer, with this amber o' meal; none o' your sharps nor dog-bran, but real Earl's barley-meal, white as an Easter smock.

[ALFRED helps, first one, then the other, in carrying the loads.]

THIRD SERF.

They won't starve, anyhow. Ten score ambers have been lodged in the King's Barn, since risingtime, along with two dozen staters of cheese.

FIRST SERF.

Aye, and more weys of bacon than I have fingers to score with, and gafolwood enow to brew as many combs of ale as 'ud drown all the Danes in Wessex.

SECOND SERF.

Trust Alfred for sousing them less wastefully nor that, before gangdays come round anew. (*To* ALFRED.) Why, thou hast more thews than any twain of us, though thou'rt not goodly grown, nor seemst fit for bearing loads. But thou liftst with a will.

ALFRED.

'Tis the will does half the work. Heave but with the heart, and no sack feels heavy.

FIRST SERF.

And here are clews of net yarn for the weaving women, that no hands hang idle in Alfred's Camp.

ALFRED.

Am I free to go, masters?

SECOND SERF.

Aye, as free as a boor may fare.

[ALFRED leaves them.]

THIRD SERF.

He's a rare hand at a pack, though we top him by a poll.

The hogs are nosing in the mast,
The tegs are in the fold,
The norland flakes are flying fast,
And o' 'tis nipping cold.

So let us to the steading slink,
 Still trolling as we gang,
 Now is the time for meat and drink,
 So let the world go hang,
  Go hang,
 So let the world go hang!

FIRST SERF.

An awry song for the lambing season, and with the cuckoo a-chuckling over the foster hedge-sparrow.

THIRD SERF.

No song's out o' season that cheers a man up. There's more warmth in an old song than in green faggots.

SECOND SERF.

Aye, and singing's a posset that suits summer and winter alike. They say Alfred the King wrote rare ditties before the Army broke out anew; though more anent spear-thrusts than tankards. But gammer rhymes are well enough for honest churls.

SCENE II

[The King's Chamber.]

ETHELNOTH.

Still, Alfred comes not.

PLEGMUND.

     He is sure to come
Ere to the socket burns this rushlight down.
He never wantoned with his word, nor now
Will prove untrue to it.

ETHELNOTH.

     Not if he live,
Nor if he still be free to come. But how
If eyes as searching as his own have stripped
From off his kingly gait the peasant's smock,
And even now within the Danish lines
He dwells a bondman.

ETHELRED.

     Out! They will as soon
Twine leathern thongs about the nimble air

As net him in their toils. Ne'er would they guess
There moves the man so reckless as to range
Unshielded 'mid his foes, scenting their trail
Close as a sleuth-hound.

[ALFRED enters.]

      Ethelnoth, the King!

[They make obeisance.]

ALFRED.

Yes, I am back, my wistful friends, but not
Ere I have marked where the false Guthrum folds
His savage flock, and whither next he wends,
Seeking fresh pasture; aye, and every track,
Here through the forest, there along the stream,
And clear beyond between the dimpled downs,
That, twisting hither and thither, will lead at length
To covert hollow, whence, with God for guide,
We may upon their present fastness spring,
And send them flying heartless as the wind,
Over the waste they have made.

ETHELNOTH.

     Thank Heaven! you are safe,
Nor for such wayward danger paid with life.

ALFRED.

And if I had! 'Tis not for length of days,
No, but for breadth of days that we should crave.
Life is God's gift for godlike purposes.
'Tis the mere die we play with; that which counts
Is the high stake of honour that we throw for,
And for such worthy gamesters Heaven provides.
Not in safe coffer should we lock our lives,
But put them out to peril, that our sons
May be the richer for the stake we won.
Withal, my shrewd Archbishop, 'tis allowed,
When dangerous duty doth not bid us spend
Life without thought or reckoning, 'tis so short,
Well must it be to use it thriftily;
So for your helpful hands is further work,
To eke out mine, still hampered by the sword.
Aid me; nay, mend me; for my lesser skill
Needs your large craft. Pope Gregory's Pastoral,
We call his Hindbook in our English tongue,
Worcester's good Bishop, Werefrith, will revise.
And I myself must follow, when I may,
Wulfstan and Othere through those norward seas
Whence came our fathers on their flashing oars,

And with their Finnish voyages enrich
The pages of Orosius. Unto you
The harder task, to render faithfully
The *Consolations of Philosophy*,
Where I have missed what sage Boethius means.
O Plegmund! Plegmund! Sore is it to scan,
As yesternight I did, in Alcuin's verse,
The list of Latin texts once housed in York,
The envy of the Frankish Emperor,
Great Charles himself, now wandering on the winds,
Or fuel for the fire of these rude Danes,
But all of them to be some day replaced
By God's good help and yours, and written plain
In Saxon speech for English boys to read,
And thereby understand, though, unlike me,
They may not journey thither, that which Rome
Did and still does to better man. But now,
The dwindling rushlight in the lanthorn shows
We must unto the Witan. Ethelnoth,
Come to my side, and you too, Ethelred,
Both craftier with the sword than with the pen,
And help me both with presence and with voice
To rouse my people from their peaceful hives,
And make them swarm for battle!

SCENE III

[*The Witanagemote. Alfred, wearing a circlet of gold round his head, and bearing in his hand a wand, is seated on a high oaken settle, with Edward standing on his right. Round him are his Reeves, Thanes, and chief Ealdormen; Plegmund, Archbishop of Canterbury; Werefrith, Bishop of Worcester, and Grimbald, his Mass-priest. In the enclosed space are congregated the lesser Ealdormen and their followers, the armed Freemen. Behind, at a little distance, stand the short-haired unarmed Serfs. The Queen and her daughter Ethelfrida, followed by a train of noble maidens, carry the mead-bowl round to the Thanes and Ealdormen.*]

FIRST FREEMAN.

He looks like Justice throned.

SECOND FREEMAN.

And such he is,
And hither will none hie to press their claim,
Save it be true; for Alfred's gaze can pierce
Through densest fogs of falsehood and uncloak
Each hireling lie.

THIRD FREEMAN.

Withal, how mild his look.
A mother's eyes are not more moist with love

Than his, when they are fixed upon his son,
The stalwart Atheling.

FOURTH FREEMAN.

      Yet is he stern
As Ethelnoth himself, if he but mark
Some blemish on a forehead unabashed.
I would as lief face God, were I to blame,
As stand, for fault stripped bare, before the King.

FIRST FREEMAN.

Can it be true that he as lettered is
As Grimbald's self?

SECOND FREEMAN.

      Aye, ever since the day
He learned the book of pictured Saxon verse
Quickest of all his brothers, he hath stored
His mind with written lore.

THIRD FREEMAN.

      I mind me, too,
How in his boyhood was there none more deft
To cope a haggard peregrine, to knit

The bewits to the bells, or smoothly swing
The feathered lure around his head until
The unseamed falcon learned to wing its way
Over the herons homing up the wind,
And, binding, rake its quarry to the ground.

FOURTH FREEMAN.

Aye, and I warrant he could still unhood
A cast, and send them flying on the chase,
As he will stoop upon the Danes, and force
Their filthy pannels to disgorge the food
Poached in our English pools.

FIRST FREEMAN.

      In every art
He shows the way. Woodcraft and masonry,
Shoesmith or wheelwright, all are one to him.
He throws the buttressed bridge across the stream,
And plans the sinewy curve of each fresh keel
That bears the roving ramparts of the realm.
Unto the goldsmith's dainty handiwork
He lends his counsel, even while he broods
On the rough shifts and sudden wants of war.
Never, like Buhred, would he quit the land,

Came every Danish oarsman oversea
To hem us in.

SECOND FREEMAN.

Hush! He anon will speak.

ALFRED (*rising*).

Ealdormen, and Thanes, and Free Men all,
Whom here I see, banded in battle-gear,
Kin of my sceptre, helpmates of my sword,
To you I come, your King and Overlord,
Offering and seeking wisdom. Let them speak,
So that they fight, both when and how they will,
And only those stand husht who bear no spear.
For 'twere unmeet that those who in a State
Wield no more worthy weapon than the tongue,
Should have or voice or share in ruling it.
In Witanagemote and Folkmote both,
More royal-rich than these marsh fastnesses,
In better days we have met. But let none think
That I am less a King, or you more base,
That of such trappings we awhile are scant
As Peace can hang about a Ruler's hearth.
For he still reigns whose mind is not dethroned,

And, though marauders ravage half his realm,
Upholds unserfed the Sceptre of his soul.
Kings there have been, aye and of Cerdic's blood,
With Woden's thunder moaning in their veins,
Who, even as Inè, doffed a doleful Crown,
Donning the cowl. I shall not do like these.
What though I found within the royal bed,
Where I had lain with this my cleanly Queen,
Littered, the farrow of a forest sow,
Should I bemoan the fashion of the world,
Tonsure the head Pope Leo's very hand
Anointed kingly, and slink hence to Rome
A niddering pilgrim? Never, while you stand
Steadfast about me! Nay, if you should leave
The Crown of Egbert fenceless on my brow,
It should not fall till I had fallen too,
And gone to God to answer for my Rule,
As every shriven soul must answer Him
Whose Sceptre doth not pass. Tell me then, now,
Free Men of Hampshire, Devon, Somerset,
Here mustered in your Hundreds, do you will
That we fare forth anew unto the field,
To put it to the proof of life and death,
If this fair isle be Guthrum's land or ours?

FREEMEN (*clashing their spears*).
Aye! Aye!

ALFRED.

You answer as beseemeth those that clung
Close to my side at Ashdune on the day
When Ethelred, my brother, now with God,
Lingered at mass, and the rough Danish King,
Barsac, along with Osbern, Harold, Frene,
And the two Sidracs, lay upon their backs,
And never stood up more; aye, and who took
Their share with me in those eight sinewy shocks
At Merton, Reading, Wilton, Englefield,
Within one year, whereby, when first I wore
The kingly crown, Guthrum and Oskytel
Swore not alone on relics of the saints,
But on their pagan bracelet smeared with blood,
In sacrifice, the pledges now they break.
Their hostages I hold, but 'tis not meet
That upon these should fall the Christian sword;
And, spared, they now fain fight upon our side,
Betraying their betrayers. But there be
Others, unfree, withal for whom Christ died,
Into whose hands I will entrust the spear,

So they will thrust for England, and your voice
Says aye to mine.

    FREEMEN (*clashing their spears*).
Aye! Aye!

    ALFRED (*to the Serfs*).
Therefore, in this free Witan, I decree,
Weaponless men, that you be weaponed now;
And, should you fall, your offspring shall be free,
And offspring's offspring, and their locks shall float
Over their necks by no base burden bowed.
Nor yet of these alone I snap the chain;
But unto you, the tonsured serfs of God,
I stretch my hand, and bid you, I your King,
To do as Toli at Kesteven did,
When Hingvar's pagan bands, with Hubba's horde,
Moved against Croyland, now alas! their prey:
The layman's sword he buckled to his frock,
And with the battle-axe avenged the Cross.
Do you as he, and with a better doom,
Reclaiming Croyland, Ely, Huntingdon,
For pious peace, such as at Glastonbury

Still happily abides. Yet, since the land
Which bred you, suckled you, and fosters now,
Hath upon all male thews this righteous toll,
More needful is it still that they whom God
Shaped to be nests and nourishers of life,
Should double now their song and suit to Heaven
For England's weal. Therefore, my Wife, depart,
With all white souls that willing wend with you,
Unto the eastern gate of Shaftesbury,
And build you there a nunnery whose vows
May win the deathless Overlord of War
To lead our van in fight, and fence our rear.
I have your leave for this, Lady and Wife,
Whom still a silent helpmate at my side,
And by that silence keeping me more strong,
I pray to have, till strength avails no more.
And, though my grandsire Egbert left his land
To those that wield the spear, and not to those
That ply the distaff, and his law stands mine,
To you, in endless token of the trust
That you have had in me, and I in you,
I do bequeathe Wantage and Athelney,
My cradle, and my refuge, in this war,
To hold as free as you have held my love.

And may the bane of Christ and all His Saints
Blind him that setteth it aside!

[The QUEEN, ETHELFRIDA, and their handmaidens, depart.
As they pass out, ASSER, followed by a group of Welsh
Chieftains, enters.]

ALFRED.

But who
Breaks in upon our Mote?

[Recognising ASSER.]

Right welcome guest!
Asser, my own true Asser, light in dark,
Friend, teacher, trusty in all thought and deed!

[ALFRED descends from his kingly settle, embraces ASSER,
and leads him to a seat at his side.]

Whence come you, and these dark outlandish men,
That hang upon your heel, as though afeard
To lose the claim of service, and to fall
Forfeit to foes? Tell them they here are safe
As at God's altar.

ASSER.

Loving Lord and King,
My pupil, yet my master, these scared men
Are gentle in their blood, of princely birth,

Sons of King Mouric, Tendyr, Hemrid, Ris,
Who now on-this-side Britain wield the rod.
They from Demetria followed me, their guide,
To crave your overlordship in their land
Against the unrulier Welsh that harry it,
Leagued with the Danish robbers of the main.

ALFRED.

Asser! to bring good tidings ever first,
You never brought me blither news than this.
Bid them be seated,—aye, more near to me,—
And tell them in their tongue, till they learn ours
Which it will be your happy lot to teach,
That in this Island there must be one lord,
One law, one speech, one bond of blood between
Saxon and Briton, and that Wales must be
Not more nor less than England, but the same.
Their will is still their own, to go or stay,
But, on the word and promise of a King,
So they will aid me to beset the foe,
And we together conquer, they shall dwell,
They and their kindred, free among their hills,
Fenced beyond heathen ravin by my sword.

[*Again addressing the Witanagemote.*]

Gone are the women. None but men stand here,
And but to men and manly ears I speak.
You know my law, whereby, one half the year,
Each one may keep his hearth and till his land,
Eschewing for that while the toll of war,
But, when the time is past, he must anew
Take shield and spear; and some of you there be
Who now afresh have claim to put these off,
And back unto their homesteads; and the law,
The law shall stand, if 'tis their will to go.
Never shall law be broken in this land,
Leastways by me: so speak who claim to go,
And nurse a liking for the coward's doom,
A grave of mire, with hurdle over it.

[*They all remain silent.*]

ALFRED.

Nay, but I will not shame you into right,
Nor in the deadly fellowship of war
Have at my side unwilling guild-brothers.
Therefore I say to all, to those that hold
Five hides of land and owe me service for it,

Earl and ceorl, tithing—hundred—man,
Franklin and yeoman, ploughman, goatherd, sower,
Hayward and woodward, all that liefer would
Earn with their sweat what they might win with blood,
You all are free to go, and in the fight
We will make boot without you. House-carles shall
Fill up the gap you leave.

FREEMEN.

We all will stay.

ALFRED.

Then pledge me in the mead-bowl, spearmen all,
Me, your host-leader! While that Ethelred,
My brother, lived, I bowed to him as King,
Though by my father's will I might have claimed
Rule over Kent; and this I did because
Twas best for England, and for England now
Is it not best I be your Overlord?

  FREEMEN (*striking their shields with their spears*).
Aye! Aye!
Alfred! Alfred!
Lord of England!
England's comfort!

England's shepherd!
England's darling!
Alfred! Alfred!

ALFRED.

Now tell them, Werefrith, that whoever falls
Fighting for England, soul-shot sure shall be,
And wend him straight from battle-doom to Christ.

[All kneel, and WEREFRITH blesses them.]

SCENE IV

[Alfred's Study. ALFRED is shaping models of long-oared boats, meant to cope with the Danish esks.]

ALFRED.

Not till the Sea hath owned us for its lord,
Will England's shore be free. Hence must we lay
Our rod along the waters till it stretch
Wide as they welter, further than they foam.
Who holds the sea, perforce doth hold the land,
And who lose that must lose the other too,
When wave on wave gleams crested with a foe,
And billows given for safety gape with doom
And ruin for the redeless. Right meseem

Stem, stern, and keel, nigh twice the bulk of those
The Frisians use, and with a sharper sweep.
God grant that I may chase them from the seas,
And gird this island with a watery belt
Not all the world in arms can cleave or cross!

[Enter the Atheling.]

EDWARD.

Unto your bidding, Father, am I come.

ALFRED.

Where were you, Edward, yesterday at noon?

EDWARD.

In Selwood Forest, in its very heart,
Hard by the clearing round the hut where dwells
The neatherd Danewulf.

ALFRED.

And why went you there?

EDWARD.

To greet the loveliest maiden in the land.
Forgive me, Sir! but oh, if you could see
How fair, how——

ALFRED.

     Hold! enough! A fault avowed
Is sooth a fault forgiven. Bating untruth,
There is no blot I could not brook in you,
Hoping to mend it. For remember, Edward!
Truth is the free man's weapon, and a lie
Makes him unfree and sinks him to the serf.
I would that in this land, which some day will
Be happier far than I or you can make it,
Truth should be deemed the first and last of virtues.
For truth is justice, fairness, fearlessness,
And is to man as honesty to woman;
And I would liefer see you hewn to death
By Pagan battle-axe than soil your lips
With craven paltering. But, Edward, Edward,
Though lust is not so base as is a lie,
It ofttimes leads thereto; and, even when
It wants that last worst shame, what bane it brings
On households and on kingdoms! Well you know
What brought the perjured Guthrum to this land,
Lured oversea by Biorn Butsecarl,
To be avenged on the adulterous King,
Northumbrian Osberht.

    [EDWARD is about to speak.]

Nay, but let me tell,
For your soul's hale, that in my own hot youth
Flesh with the spirit was so sore at war,
I prayed to God He would in kindness send
Some sickness that might chasten this base fire,
And make me rule-worthy; for he who lives
Thrall unto fleshly bondage is not fit
To be the lord of others; and God sent
A scourge so sharp, that I again besought
Some milder stroke,—not blindness, leprosy,
Nor any hurt unworthy of a King,—
And in His goodness He then laid on me
The burden that you know.

EDWARD.

Father, I swear,
My love for this fair maiden is as clean
As her unblemished soul, and I would fain,
Having your yea, still woo her for my wife.
Nay, but still hear me, you that ever were
Suffering and mild, blithesome and good to me,
Let me go fetch and bring her to your feet!
The coralled hawthorn in the wayside brake,
When Autumn winds have blown the leaves away,

Hath not the ruddy ripeness of her lips.
June's bluebells are not heavenlier than her eyes,
Nor than her cheek more dewy, and her voice,—
The woodwete's is no sweeter when it soars,
And we look up to hear it!

ALFRED.

Need is none
To tell me that. I heard it yesterday,
Between the whiles you wantoned in the wood,
And heeded not the King that crossed your path,
In tattered seeming.

EDWARD.

Your forgiveness, Father!

ALFRED.

Rise, boy! Your love is loyal; and no maid,
That, bred on English soil and fain to bide
By English hearthfire, hath not in her blood
The blur of bondage, can be held unmeet
To grace the bed and settle of a King.
But, Edward, can it be, in these mirk days,
You dally in the dreamy ways of love,

SCENE IV   ENGLAND'S DARLING   57

Now that your one fast thought by day, your one
Fond hope when moist sleep loosens all your limbs,
Should be for England! England, none but England
Clean or unclean, this is no time for love.
Where is your sword? I'll have no Atheling
Lulled in the sleek and sleepy lap of love,
When every heart-beat in his body should
Hasten the hour for death-grip with the Dane!

[Enter a Messenger.]

MESSENGER.

A Danish girl, seen slinking by the stream
Trod by your outmost watchers, hath been brought
Into the camp, and claims to see the King.

ALFRED.

Let her within.

[EDGIVA enters.]

EDGIVA.

Edward!

EDWARD (*to Edgiva*).
            The King!

[EDGIVA kneels.]

ALFRED (*to* EDWARD, *sternly*).

                              Go hence!
[EDWARD quits the King's presence.]

ALFRED.

Rise, child! But wherefore pry you in our land,
So straitened now, that all beyond it feeds
The heathen Army?

EDGIVA.

                    But I did not pry.
I am as true to Alfred and his name,
As they that roughly clutched and dragged me here,
Because of Danish bracelet round my wrist;
And, since they would not harken, but led on
My footsteps hitherward, I claimed to see
Yourself, the King, and tell you all my tale.

ALFRED.

Tell it me, then.

EDGIVA.

                    Who was it that you chid
Out of your sight?

ALFRED.

My son, the Atheling.

EDGIVA.

Oh!

[She covers her face.]

Why did he come into my lowly life,
And with his April sunshine cozen it
To blossom back to his! It was not worthy.
I pray you, let me fare unto my home,
To Danewulf and my mother, where I may
Forget him utterly, and never more
Hear words of fond untruth.

ALFRED.

Blame him not thus!
He is my son, and, never since he learned
From Saxon mother this our Saxon tongue,
Or spake or thought untruth. He loves too well,
And hence it was I drove him from your sight.

EDGIVA.

'Twas all unwitting that I gave him first
A love-tryst in the forest. Had I known!

But now meseems I know not what I know,
Save that I never will behold him more.
Nay, be a King! and send me to my home!

ALFRED.

We'll think of that to-morrow. For to-night,
You needs must lie in Athelney. But, child,
What sought you when our wardens, overwise,
As witlessness oft is, enforced you here?

EDGIVA.

It was the path whereby he went when last
He looked farewell, and so I trod the place,
Because it seemed to bring me nearer to him;
And, as I did so, luckless that I am,
I dropped and lost upon the river bank,
Or maybe in the stream, the crystal token
Given me by hoary wanderer who had sought
Rest in our hut, and promised, should I seek
His dwelling with that earnest, he would teach me
To spell and read, and make me learned and wise.
Now is it lost, and everything is lost,
And I shall know nor love nor learning now.

ALFRED.

Would you that withered master know again?

EDGIVA.

Sooth, that I should! I never can forget
His look, his voice. His speech was like to yours,
But he was gone in years, and on his brow
Their snows had drifted.

ALFRED.

     Maiden, it was I,
Whose business 'tis to learn what mischief may
Be brewing on our borders, so awhile
Misfeatured thus; and you have nothing lost,
Saving the jewel, easily forgone,
And somewhere lost for other days to find,
Time-token of the trouble England bore,
And, bearing, yet will better. I myself,
True to my word, will teach your tongue to read,
And you teach Edward more than thus you learn,—
Since household lore the truest wisdom is,—
When War's loud shuttle shall have woven peace,
And in this England all who love may live

As safe as nest of whinchat in the brake.
But, child, not now, not now! For never think,
Until the howling pack of Pagan wolves
Are flogged to heel or scattered oversea,
To lift and lay your arms about his neck,
Whose service lies elsewhere! What ho! without.

[An attendant enters.]

Unto our Lady lead this guest, and say
It is the bidding of the King she be
With the handmaidens pillowed for the night.

END OF ACT II

ACT III

SCENE I

[The Fens north-east of Athelney. The ATHELING and EDGIVA on the water; EDWARD rowing, EDGIVA steering.]

EDGIVA.

It might be March, not May, so crisp the wind
Curls the sleek water, and besets the keel,
Driving it slantwise.

EDWARD.

        Then, sweet, keep her straight.
For, says the King, pondering on mightier things,
Face a head gust and it will steady you.
See! 'tis nor May nor March, but April's self,
That runs along the ripples of the mere,
Sunning gray wrinkles into golden smiles. . . .
Look! look!

EDGIVA.

What was't?

EDWARD.

                A feeding kingfisher
Jewelled the air a moment, and is gone.

EDGIVA.

As you are going!

EDWARD.

             Nay, sweet, not for long.
Let us but root the heathen from the isle,
And then once more we many a time and oft
Will in the dark-green gloamings of moist May
Link hands in silence.

EDGIVA.

              Can you hit the spot
Where we must meet the King?

EDWARD.

                   Aye, to a rood.
'Tis hard beyond where now the wild swans breed:

She with husht pinions furled upon the nest,
He tacking fierce, and shrilling through his sails
Against intruding footstep.

EDGIVA.

Have a care!
The water waxeth shallower, and ahead
The reedmace stouter grows.

EDWARD.

I mind them well.
How often have I crushed their crackling stems,
Sered by the wind and manacled in ice,
When first we came to crouch in Athelney!
There's not a tangle in this stubborn world
I had not pushed through then, for straight my will
Was straining to your threshold! O, how long
Remorseful Winter, wishing to be Spring,
Kept feebly slipping back from sun to cloud,
From bud to snowflake! Now 'tis May! 'tis May!
The Mother-month that fosters all things good,
And, with the white renewal of the thorn,
Arrays our hearts for battle!

EDGIVA.

> Not for me!
Nay, but I would not have it otherwise.
Love England first, Edgiva afterward,
Till Peace shall make them twin. Why hath the King
Laid this great meed on my unworth, that now
We wend together unto Guthrum's camp,
Minstrel and daughter? I am sore afeard,
Not of the danger,—danger there is none
With him to lead,—no, but of his high thoughts
And my mean mind to mate them.

EDWARD.

> Have no fear.
Though low unto the lofty may not reach,
The lofty to the low doth easy stoop:
Beside, my father loves you.

EDGIVA.

> For your sake.

EDWARD.

Nay, but I know he loves you for your own;
And sure in love is neither high nor low,

But even only. More : he needs your help,
In that vexed country that you roamed a child
Ere Danewulf changed his lord, and came to dwell
Nigher to Athelney; where Deverel dips
Dark underground to suckle Wiley's stream,
And Egbert's Stone remains a mark unmoved
By war or time.

EDGIVA.

How well I can recall
Each runnel, thicket, clearing, garth, and stead,
Lowland and upland, dimple in the hills,
As free from fear as I who gazed at them.
To think that I should live to help the King!
There is a lofty sorrow in his gaze,
Like to the moon, high up in Heaven alone.

EDWARD.

Be you the star tending his loneliness.

EDGIVA.

I never could be that, but sometimes hope
He may deign weep, that I may stay his tears.

EDWARD.

Nay, never think to see him weep or wail!
Like clouds that are not low enough for rain,
His grief is far too high to fall in tears.
But now, please Heaven, his woe shall roll away,
And only sunshine sit on Alfred's brow.
But hush! we near the place. By Nicor's Thorn
The King awaits me. Bide you by the bank
Till I wend back to you.

> [He leaps from the boat, fastens it to the shore, helps Edgiva to land, then leaves her.]

SCENE II

[Nicor's Thorn.]

ALFRED (*addressing* EDWARD).

Hold fast by that. Bring but the best to front,
And keep the unsteady well in hand behind.
'Tis not the biggest udder gives most milk;
And with a trusty handful one may deal
A deadlier stroke than with a land in arms.
Husband these likewise, and ferment their hearts
With eagerness themselves to rise to best,

By showing them what manhood ripe can do.
Our Saxon spearmen you may trust to stand,
Though falls their lord.   Yourself must lead the Celts,
And they will then make merry mock of death.
But, on the way, be lord of their loose wills,
And keep them silent as the disciplined stars :
Nor let them thunder till you've lightened, lest
The foe, forewarned, find shelter from the bolt.
Be mindful, too, to leave no tell-tale trail.
Learn wisdom from the blind and witless mole,
That self-discovering burrower that upheaves
The ground wherethrough he travels, and for that
Is easy trapped.   Guthrum and Oskytel
Yet lie at Ethandune, keeping no watch,
But waste the weeks in rest and rioting,
Deeming I still am fast in Athelney.
Edgiva knows each winding of the ways
That creep unto their camp.   Fear not for us,
But do my bidding to the uttermost.
Hear you nought more, be sure that, when the sun
Hath thrice upon the heathen Army set,
We twain shall be within.   So, when the night
Throbs unto dawn, and the May moon turns pale
Because her lord is coming, then shrill loud

With noise of battle, and strike straight where waves
The unclean Raven over Guthrum's tent.
Till then, farewell! Remember Who you are,
And Who you *will* be! Mereward wend you now
Unto Edgiva. Dally not, but bend
Hither her feet. Then swift unto your oars,
And speed where all that's best in England waits you.
God edge your sword!

SCENE III

EDWARD.

Nay, you must wend alone. The King is stern,
And bids me speed. One kiss, and then farewell.

[He leaps into the boat.]

EDGIVA.

If you are slain!

EDWARD.

       Then we shall meet in Heaven!
If not, keep tryst with love at Ethandune.

SCENE IV

[In Selwood Forest. ALFRED teaching EDGIVA to read.]

ALFRED.

Now must we up and forward. You have threshed
Enough to-day to garner till to-morrow.

EDGIVA.

I would that I were not so slow of wit.

ALFRED.

And I were happy if my people could
Learn half as sharply. Well, they shall, some day.
But in these cloudy times men's thoughts fly low,
And soar not mindward. . . .
How I remember my dear Mother bringing
Unto my brothers and myself a book,
Saying it should be his who spelled it first;
And by God's pleasure, fell the book to me,—
Too late a scholar! No such friend as books.
For they with unreproachful looks and lips
Bear with our going, greet us when we come,
Misunderstood bewail not, ne'er upbraid

Though we be dull, and teach without a rod.
When you shall sit below your sceptred lord,
Lead him to honour books, and those who write them,
For to his people an unlettered King
Is as a lanthorn lacking of its light.

EDGIVA.

I will be mindful. Tell me more of Rome,
Whereof we read but now.

ALFRED.

                    I was a child,
With stammering tongue and half-awakened gaze,
When Ethelred, my father, now with God,
Bore me to Rome. But, an I close mine eyes,
I can behold, in dream as clear as day,
Its hills, and all the wonders throned upon them.
Rome once was Overlord to all the world,
But not for Empire now, nay, for bare life,
Is ofttimes hard beset: a fallen Rome,
Yet awful in its fall; bemocked and scourged,
Humbled and thorn-crowned, as meseems is fit
For Christ's own city, mastering still mankind
By the rood-token of His martyrdom.

My father gave a hundred mancuses
For oil wherewith to keep the lamp alight
By Peter's tomb from Easter Eve till dawn,
As I too will, when better days shall come.
For 'tis my wish to see, in this strong land,
A manly State wed to a wifely Church,
The helpmeet this, but that one still the lord.
For, as the woman, so too is the Church
Of a diviner nature, but on earth
They should but meekly counsel, then obey.

[They walk on in silence.]

ALFRED.

Wot you the hour?

EDGIVA.

It must be long past noon,
Because the shepherd's weather-wise hath shut,
As doth the goatsbeard in the waning year.

ALFRED.

That is a lore not to be had from books,
Withal more helpful. Know you all the flowers?

EDGIVA.

All were too many. Some there be I know,
Taught me by Danewulf and my foster-mother.
She tells their uses, he their home and name.
Is that a wound you have upon your hand?

ALFRED.

'Tis but a scratch I haply got that day
I cheered me by your hearth.

EDGIVA.

                Nay, show it me.
Lay but the plantain-leaf upon the wound,
By Danewulf waybread cleped, 'twill cure it straight.

ALFRED.

There's nothing wasteful in this housewife world,
Would men themselves be heedful. I have heard
Cider gone sour will scour the foul egg white.

EDGIVA.

I've seen my mother do't a score of times.

ALFRED.

Tell me what else she doth with leaves and simples.

EDGIVA.

With pewterwort she burnishes the pans,
Makes lye of betony to soothe the brow,
And healing salve from early primroses.
She steeps for Danewulf leaves of ladysmock,
For they keep strong the heart; fresh woodruff soaks
To brew cool drink, and keep away the moth;
And, in the month when earth and sky are one,
Squeezes the bluebell 'gainst the adder's bite.
With windflower honey are my tresses smoothed,
My freckles with the speedwell's juices washed,
And sleepy breath made sweet with galingale.

ALFRED.

Nay, you should leave the freckles, since begot
By sun and wind, an honourable birth;
And Edward in his love-dream swears you are
As freckled as the foxglove, and as fair.

EDGIVA.

What, my dear lord, is that?

ALFRED.

      Nay, but you know it.
Look! there is one, half-blown before its time.

EDGIVA.

We call that thimble-flower.

ALFRED.

A better name,
As all names are, when given by simple lips.
How call you this?

EDGIVA.

We call it golden-withy.
This is bog-asphodel the Danish Jarls
Cull, so they say, to dye their yellow hair.
And this is Baldmoyne.

ALFRED.

From great Balder named,
The son of Odin.

EDGIVA.

Which, when steeped with hop,
Makes bright and brisk strong ale.

ALFRED.

Now name me this.

EDGIVA.

Milkwort, or gang-flower.

ALFRED.

Which the learnëd call
Rogation-Flower.

EDGIVA.

And this? This is the spearmint
That steadies giddiness, and that the consound,
Whereby the lungs are easëd of their grief.
The eyebright this, whereof, when steeped in wine,
I now must eat, as every learner should,
Because it strengthens mindfulness.

ALFRED.

Daughter mine,
You have as much to teach as to be taught;
Nor let new learning drive old lore away.
Rashly I spoke: There is a better friend,
A better, and a truer, even than books.
'Tis with us now, God's plainly written page.
For learned and simple, all may read who will.

SCENE V

[Evening in the Forest.]

EDGIVA.

The goldings by the brooklet all are closed.
'Twill soon be nightfall.

ALFRED.

    And, like them, your lids
Droop on your eyes. 'Tis time for you to rest.

EDGIVA.

First let me smooth for you a mossy bed,
Under this oak.

ALFRED.

    Think not, my child, of me;
For I am wakeful, and there yet is light
Whereby to read a little. But your limbs
Are fain to doff the heavy load of day,
And sink upon their weariness. Lie there,
Within the hollow of that puckered yew,
Whose boughs hath fashioned many a Saxon bow.

EDGIVA.

They say the Virgin Mother sought its shade,
Fleeing to Egypt; so no bolt will smite
Its hallowed trunk.

    [She falls asleep.]

ALFRED.
    Already doth she dream,
Way-weary child.

   [He places a posy of cowslips in her hand.]

    These sleepy cowslip bells
Will keep her dream-lids drowsy till the dawn.

 * * * * * *

How many hands it takes to build a State!
First there be those that shape and drive the share,
Yoke the meek oxen, fold and milk the ewes,
Hunt hart and boar and buck, harpoon the whale,
With cunning gin and bait ensnare the fowl,
From well-tanned fells weave hose and bridle-thongs,
Pouches and hide-vats,—skilled in toil and craft.
Then come the worthier sort that bear the shield,
Fear only God, and never show their backs
Though faced by spears a hundredfold their own.

Last but not least are those that watch and pray,
For under God it is we work and war.
All these there be, and they are at my side,
To fashion England. What it lacks is learning:
And o' how slow to learn is this stark stock,
Stark but unshapely, and with dullard ears
For sound and sense and soul of things unseen!
To every Bishop in the land, when once
The Danish Raven flickers, must I send
A copy of Pope Gregory's Pastoral,
With golden seal worth fifty mancuses,
And every English boy must read and con
The Chronicle of this his cradle-land,
Growing apace and nigh upon our time,
That tells him whence he came, and what those did
Whose deeds are in his veins. But, above all,
All men must learn its minstrelsy, and lift
Their hearts above the ground on wings of song.
For Song it is that spans the mighty world,
Brings the far near, lends light where all is dark,
Gives sorrow sweetness, and helps man to live
And die more nobly!

END OF ACT III

ACT IV

SCENE I

[The Camp of G<small>UTHRUM</small> at Ethandune. G<small>UTHRUM</small>, O<small>SKYTEL</small>, and their J<small>ARLS</small> are feasting in G<small>UTHRUM</small>'s tent.]

OSKYTEL.

Out of the skull of the foe the mead smacks sweet.
Taste of it, Guthrum.

GUTHRUM (*drinking*).

     Honey-sweet and strong!
For ale-feasts is there no such land as this,
And now 'tis ours to brew with. Do you mind
The day we fired the shrine at Huntingdon,
And supped amid the smoke? I see them now,
Lean shavelings huddled round about the shrine,

Clutching the silver beakers set with gems,
And yielding but with life the shining robes,
Woven of silk and gold, that in their coffers
Lay thick as leaves fresh ruddled by the frost.

OSKYTEL.

Aye, but at Lindsey was there fatter fare.
Your shrivelled friar is well enough to slay,
But worthless after slaying. Buxom maids,
To while away the weariness of peace,
And fair-haired boys to hand the mead-bowl round,
These are the boons of battle!

GUTHRUM.

      This to Woden!
Whose day will dawn with morrow! This to Thor,
Who hammers out the thunder and the flash,
And slays the dragon!

OSKYTEL.

     This to boar-helmed Freyr,
The sender of the needfire and the rain!
   [Turning to the JARLS.]
Why quaff you not?

FIRST JARL.

    Because of Weird at hand.
Ask them that read the staves.   This crimson-dawn,
The beechen slips on the white cloth spelled out
The runes of death.

SECOND JARL.

    And the Shieldmaidens fled
Dim to the wood.

THIRD JARL.

    Aye, and the snow-white steeds,
Lashed to the holy chariot, neighed of doom,
Then reared and snorted backward to the stall.

FIRST JARL.

I mind me of the day my lord me gave
Folkright and homestead, and I will not now
Hold back if need befall him, for unmeet
It were that I should homeward bear my shield.
But woeful are the lots.

SECOND JARL.

    I mind the time
I in the timbered beer-hall pledged my lord,

When gave he me both helm and ring, that I
Would pay him back my war-gear at his need.
So surely will I. But the runes are foul.

GUTHRUM.

We know it, trusty Jarls! You all speak sooth.
The ebon Raven which the daughters three
Of Regnor Lodbrog in one morning wove
For Hingvar and for Hubba, will not flap
Its wings for war, but droopeth listlessly,
Forewarning rout. So will we not now fight,
But hang our axes on the wall till Thor
Shine on their faces. Meanwhile, let us feast
Blithe in the land we have won.

*"I trust my sword, I trust my steed:
But most I trust myself at need."*

He's no true Jarl that doth not drink with me.

FOURTH JARL.

An agëd gleeman, with his daughter, craves
To cheer the night with song. His thews hang loose,
His back is bent like to a bow that keeps,
Unstrung, the bias of its former strain,

And wan as winter is his flaky hair.
But the unwedded helpmeet at his side,
A very bud of freshly-burgeoned May,
Vows in his voice that manhood lingers still,
And he can sing of war, and love, and aught
That's bidden of his craft.

     GUTHRUM.

        Then bring him in.

SCENE II

[ALFRED and EDGIVA are led in, and placed, side by side, on a high settle near the opening of the tent, opposite GUTHRUM and OSKYTEL.]

     OSKYTEL.

Give him to quaff, out of this cup of mine.
He'll troll the lustier if first warmed with ale.

     GUTHRUM !

Now for brave singing !

     ALFRED.

In the Beginning when, out of darkness,
  The Earth, the Heaven,
  The stars, the seasons,

The mighty mainland,
And whale-ploughed water,
By God the Maker
Were formed and fashioned,
Then God made England.

He made it shapely
With land-locked inlets,
And gray-green nesses;
With rivers roaming
From fair-leafed forests
Through windless valleys,
Past plain and pasture,
To sloping shingle:
Thus God made England.

Then like to the long-backed bounding billows,
That foam and follow
In rolling ridges,
Before and after,
To bluff and headland,
Hither there tided
The loose-limbed Briton,
The lording Roman,

> *And strong on his oars the sea-borne Saxon,*
> *And now the Norsemen*
> *Who hard with Alfred*
> *Wrestle for England.*

GUTHRUM.

How lustily he trolls! A glee like this
Would stave off bane and death.

OSKYTEL.

Look on him now!
He gleams as though to-day and yesterday
Had with to-morrow trysted in his gaze.
A Seer! A Seer! Jarls! Drink unto the Seer!

JARLS.

Aye, and to his fair daughter must we quaff!

ALFRED.

> *But onward and forward,*
> *In far days fairer,*
> *I see this England*
> *Made one and mighty:*
> *Mighty and master*
> *Of all within it.*

Mighty and master
Of men high-seated,
Of free-necked labour,
Lowland and upland,
And corn and cattle,
And ploughland peaceful,
Of happy homesteads
That warmly nestle
In holt and hollow.
This is the England,
In fair days forward,
I see and sing of.

GUTHRUM.

And who shall have this England?

JARLS.

Aye, who shall have this England?

ALFRED.

Then, mighty and master of all within her,
Of Celt and Briton,
Angle and Frisian,
Saxon and Norseman,

Shall England plough, like the whale and walrus,
  The roaring ridges
  Of foam-necked water,
  With long-oared warships
  And keels high-beakëd;
  And never a foeman,
  Eastward or westward,
  Shall dare to raven
  Her salt-sea inlets,
  Her grim gray nesses,
But, swift at the sight of her rearing cradles,
  Shall scud and scatter,
  Like wild geese fleeing
  'Twixt wave and welkin,
Away from the dread of the shrilling weapons
  Of foam-fenced England!

OSKYTEL.

But who shall have this England?

GUTHRUM.

Aye, who shall have this England?

[A horn sounds, and shouts are heard without. ALFRED throws off his disguise, stands erect in kingly garb, and, drawing his sword, exclaims :]

ALFRED.

Alfred shall have this England!
Lord Christ shall have this England!

[EDWARD, ETHELRED, ETHELNOTH, and a body of the King's Thanes, rush in. ALFRED disarms GUTHRUM, who has struck at him with his battle-axe. EDWARD fells and disarms OSKYTEL, and the Jarls that do not yield are slain.]

EDWARD.

The Golden Dragon floats o'er Ethandune.
We broke upon the Army in its sleep,
And bound the weaponless. Those that awoke
With battle-axe in grip, the ruffled vulture,
The swarthy raven, and the sallow kite,
Are rawly tattering with their tawny nibs;
And wealden wolves will batten on the rest.

ALFRED (*to Guthrum*).

Now yet again the Lord of War hath placed
Your life within my hands. Forfeited once,
I gave it back to you, when first you swore,
Upon our sacred tokens and your own,
To dwell in peace with me and mine for aye.
Your hostages I held: I hold you now.

Why should the sword not fall upon your neck?
But, since Lord Christ hath won this fight for me,
And He is pitiful, I fain would spare
And leave you free within East Anglia,
But owning me for King and Overlord,
If you can tend me tighter pledge than that
Forsworn and broken.

GUTHRUM.

                Bind me, an you will,
To Christ your King, who henceforth shall be mine.
For He is mightier than our Gods, as you
Are mightier than our Vikings!

ALFRED.

                Henceforth then,
Live, like to us, at peace within this land,
Our brothers, not our bane; our were-gild yours,
Our foe your foe, our feud your feud, and you,
No less than we, English in name and heart.
Up from the mouth of Thames along the Lea
To where the Ouse leads on to Watling Street
Hold you the land, but at my bidding still
If need should rise.   Beyond, is Mercia;

Which Ethelred, my sister's trusty lord,
Under my rod will rule. You, Ethelnoth,
Rebuild and strengthen London, and make good
Our name along the twistings of the Thames;
While Werefrith, helped by Plegmund, shall renew
God's House at Winchester. Thanes, Freemen,
    Friends,
Let each one strive to quit him worthily.
For me, I have no other wish on earth,
Save to leave long remembrance after me
Of something done for England!

    OSKYTEL (*gazing hard on Edgiva, who is standing by*
        Edward).
What is this token, wound about your wrist?
Are you Sweyne's daughter? my dead comrade's child,
Whom we left, motherless, within the fork
Of a high wychelm, thinking soon to fetch
Her safely from that cradle, on the day
That Ethelwulf and Wulfheard, Saxon Thanes,
Beset our Jarls, and over the White Horse
Drove us in headlong rout across the stream.

        EDWARD.

Noble I knew her!

ALFRED.

Nobly wed her then!
And when God calls me to Himself, for men
Know not how long or little they will stay,
May offspring worthy of your fair love and you,
Saxon with Dane, hand down the English Throne!

ETHELRED (*bursting into the tent*).

Great news, my Lord! The ships you bade us build
Full nigh on twice the length of pagan esks,
At Swanage on the robber swan-necks rode,
And wedged them through the waves. Their splintered planks
Are weltering with the seaweed; their snapped oars,
Like to their carcases, the gurgling ooze
Sucks down, then belches forth again, to rot
Upon the brackish furrows of the brine.

ALFRED.

Now praised be God! for this is news indeed,
And Swanage crowns us more than Ethandune.
In this strong Isle sequestered by the sea
From tread outlandish, victory upon ground
Our own to keep or lose, is half defeat;

For why on English soil should foe's foot stand?
The battlemented Sea will beat him off,
So we but man it, and our bounding prows
Scatter him flying deathward o'er the foam,
Like loose leaves harried by autumnal wind.
Aye, and in those bright bodings that high Heaven
Vouchsafes at times to man, my ken foresees
That, once this land inviolably free
From threat without, its billow-suckled breed,
Yearning beyond the narrow bonds of birth,
Wherever shine the stars or rolls the tide,
Will lay their lordship on the waves, and be
Rulers and rovers of the widening world.

ALL.

Long live Alfred!
Long rule Alfred!
England's Comfort,
England's Shepherd,
England's Oarsman,
England's Darling!

END OF ACT IV

THE PASSING OF MERLIN

The following Poem appeared in *The Times* of
October 7th 1892.

THE PASSING OF MERLIN

> I am Merlin,
> And I am dying,
> I am Merlin
> Who follow The Gleam.
> TENNYSON'S *Merlin and The Gleam.*

I.

MERLIN has gone—has gone!—and through the land
The melancholy message wings its way;
To careless-ordered garden by the bay,
Back o'er the narrow strait to island strand,
Where Camelot looks down on wild Broceliand.

II.

Merlin has gone, Merlin the Wizard who found,
In the Past's glimmering tide, and hailed him King,
Arthur, great Uther's son, and so did sing
The mystic glories of the Table Round,
That ever its name will live so long as Song shall sound.

III.

Merlin has gone, Merlin who followed the Gleam,
And made us follow it; the flying tale
Of the Last Tournament, the Holy Grail,
And Arthur's Passing; till the Enchanter's dream
Dwells with us still awake, no visionary theme.

IV.

To-day is dole in Astolat, and dole
In Celidon the forest, dole and tears.
In Joyous Gard blackhooded lean the spears:
The nuns of Almesbury sound a mournful toll,
And Guinevere kneeling weeps, and prays for
    Merlin's soul.

V.

A wailing cometh from the shores that veil
Avilion's island valley; on the mere,
Looms through the mist and wet winds weeping blear
A dusky barge, which, without oar or sail,
Fades to the far-off fields where falls nor snow nor
    hail.

VI.

Of all his wounds He will be healëd now,
Wounds of harsh time and vulnerable life,
Fatigue of rest and weariness of strife,
Doubt and the long deep questionings that plough
The forehead of age but bring no harvest to the brow.

VII.

And there He will be comforted; but we
Must watch, like Bedivere, the dwindling light
That slowly shrouds Him darkling from our sight.
From the great deep to the great deep hath He
Passed, and, if now He knows, is mute eternally.

VIII.

From Somersby's ivied tower there sinks and swells
A low slow peal, that mournfully is rolled
Over the long gray fields and glimmering wold,
To where, 'twixt sandy tracts and moorland fells,
Remembers Locksley Hall his musical farewells.

IX.

And many a sinewy youth on Cam to-day
Suspends the dripping oar and lets his boat
Like dreaming water-lily drift and float,
While murmuring to himself the undying lay
That haunts the babbling Wye and Severn's dirgeful bay.

X.

The bole of the broad oak whose knotted knees
Lie hidden in the fern of Sumner Place,
Feels stirred afresh, as when Olivia's face
Lay warm against its rind, though now it sees
Not Love but Death approach, and shivers in the breeze.

XI.

In many a Vicarage garden, dense with age,
The haunt of pairing throstles, many a grange
Moated against the assault and siege of change,
Fair eyes consult anew the cherished Sage,
And now and then a tear falls blistering the page.

XII.

April will blossom again, again will ring
With cuckoo's call and yaffel's flying scream,
And in veiled sleep the nightingale will dream,
Warbling as if awake. But what will bring
His sweet note back ? He mute, it scarcely will be
    Spring.

XIII.

The Seasons sorrow for Him, and the Hours
Droop, like to bees belated in the rain.
The unmoving shadow of a pensive pain
Lies on the lawn and lingers on the flowers,
And sweet and sad seem one in woodbine-woven
    bowers.

XIV.

In English gardens fringed with English foam,
Or girt with English woods, He loved to dwell,
Singing of English lives in thorp or dell,
Orchard or croft ; so that, when now we roam
Through them, and find Him not, it scarcely feels
    like home.

XV.

And England's glories stirred Him as the swell
Of bluff winds blowing from Atlantic brine
Stirs mightier music in the murmuring pine.
Then sweet notes waxed to strong within his shell,
And bristling rose the lines, and billowy rose and fell.

XVI.

So England mourns for Merlin, though its tears
Flow not from bitter source that wells in vain,
But kindred rather to the rippling rain
That brings the daffodil sheath and jonquil spears,
When Winter weeps away and April reappears.

XVII.

For never hath England lacked a voice to sing
Her fairness and her fame, nor will she now.
Silence awhile may brood upon the bough,
But shortly once again the Isle will ring
With wakening winds of March and rhapsodies of Spring.

XVIII.

From Arthur unto Alfred, Alfred crowned
Monarch and Minstrel both, to Edward's day,
From Edward to Elizabeth, the lay
Of valour and love hath never ceased to sound,
But Song and Sword are twin, indissolubly bound.

XIX.

Nor shall in Britain Taliessin tire
Transmitting through his stock the sacred strain.
When fresh renown prolongs Victoria's Reign,
Some patriot hand will sweep the living lyre,
And prove, with native notes, that Merlin was his sire.

THE END.

Printed by R. & R. CLARK, LIMITED, *Edinburgh.*

THE POETICAL WORKS

OF

ALFRED AUSTIN
Poet Laureate

LYRICAL POEMS. One vol. Crown 8vo. 5s.

NARRATIVE POEMS. One vol. Crown 8vo. 5s.

THE TOWER OF BABEL: A Celestial Love Drama. One vol. Crown 8vo. 5s.

SAVONAROLA: A Tragedy. One vol. Crown 8vo. 5s.

THE HUMAN TRAGEDY. One vol. Crown 8vo. 5s.

PRINCE LUCIFER. One vol. Crown 8vo. 5s.

FORTUNATUS THE PESSIMIST. One vol. Crown 8vo. 5s.

MADONNA'S CHILD. One vol. Fcap. 8vo. 2s. 6d. net.

MACMILLAN AND CO., LONDON.

[Turn over.

Crown 8vo. 3*s.* 6*d.*

ENGLISH LYRICS

A SELECTION FROM THE LYRICAL POEMS OF ALFRED AUSTIN

EDITED, WITH A PREFACE,

BY WILLIAM WATSON

EXTRACT FROM THE PREFACE

"A nobly filial love of Country, and a tenderly passionate *love of the country*—these appear to me the two dominant notes of this volume. The phrases themselves stand for things widely different, but it seems fated that the things themselves should be found present together or together absent. . . . Our literature prior to Lord Tennyson contains no such full utterance of this dual passion, this enthusiasm of nationality underlying an intimate and affectionate knowledge of every bird that makes an English summer melodious, and every flower that sweetens English air; and it seems to me that if the question be asked, 'Who among the poets of a later generation can be said to share with Lord Tennyson the quality of being in this double sense English through and through?' any competent person trying to answer the question honestly will find the name of the author of this volume of *English Lyrics* the first to rise to his lips.

"Mr. Alfred Austin would seem to love England none the less, but rather the more, because he has also felt the spell of other countries with a keenness only possible in natures which present a wide surface to impressions. In *The Human Tragedy* he has projected himself by imaginative sympathy into the very life and spirit of the land

'Where Milan's spires go up to heaven like prayer,'

and

'Where once-proud Genoa sits beside the sea.'

EXTRACT FROM THE PREFACE

But that very poem, full of Italian feeling and aglow with Italian colour as it is, opens with a chant of English springtime which is assuredly hard to match outside its author's own vernal verse. As pictures to hang up in one's mental gallery side by side with the exquisite 'spring' of *The Human Tragedy*, perhaps one would choose the autumn landscapes in *Love's Widowhood*, though some of these are harder to detach without loss or injury from their setting, being not so much examples of deliberate description as of that rarer art by which a poem is saturated with autumnal sentiment till the lines seem to rustle with fallen foliage, and their melody to come muffled through an indolent September haze.

"Mr. Alfred Austin may in a special sense be styled the laureate of the English seasons, for he seems equally happy whether he be championing our northern April against the onslaught of a critic who had fallen foul of that best-abused of months in an evening journal, or colouring his verse with the gravely gorgeous pigments of the time when nature seems sunk in reverie, and leaf by leaf the pageant of verdure crumbles down, or painting for us (*etching* would perhaps be the better word) the likeness of earth in that interval of apparent quiescence or suspended life, when her pinched and haggard features have put on an ascetic severity, and she seems to be doing penance alike for her summer revelries and the extravagant pomps of autumn,—when

> 'in the sculptured woodland's leafless aisles
> The robin chants the vespers of the year.'

Thus it is that he seems among modern poets especially and saliently English, in the sense in which most of our best singers, from Chaucer onwards, have been English; a sense implying neither insularity nor prejudice nor any resistance of foreign impressions, but an out-of-door breeziness and freedom such as bring with them an almost physical consciousness of enlargement and space. None have imbibed more deeply than he the spirit of Italy, or surrendered themselves with franker gusto to the intoxication of southern air, yet when he comes back to these shores he comes back

> 'Blessing the brave bleak land where he was born,'

somewhat as a loiterer in courts and palaces might return with a newly-quickened affection to the hearth and rafters of an unforgotten rustic

EXTRACT FROM THE PREFACE

home. Whatsoever is worthily and nobly English is endeared to him by every early association and innate prepossession, but most of all the older and simpler modes of our national life, when still unmenaced with displacement by less comely and more mechanical conditions. The old-world charm and grace which yet ennoble the labours of tilth and husbandry; the kindly charities of rustic good-neighbourhood and human relations of cottage and farm and hall ; the unique blending of stateliness and homeliness which makes the rural abodes of the gentle class in this country seem the most delectable of possible dwelling-places ;—all these things are found mirrored in this poet's verse, not with any conventional idealisation, but with such simple faithfulness to the fact as is natural in one to whom the fact is as familiar as it is dear. And together with these things, but oftener felt as an implicit presence than overtly uttered, is the underlying sentiment of England's greatness on the historic and constitutional side, the enthusiasm for whatever is splendid and heroic in 'our rude island-story,' the chivalric passion of loyalty and allegiance which flames up in quick resentment if any affront be offered to the object of its devotion — as witness the noble sonnet 'To England,' written at the moment when the action of a great British minister, in despatching our Fleet to the Black Sea and calling out the Reserves, checked the advance of Russia upon Constantinople.

> 'Men deemed thee fallen, did they?'

he asks—

> 'Not wholly shorn of strength, but vainly strong,

and lapped in the luxury of a fool's paradise, because secure, in the last resort,

> 'Behind the impassable fences of the foam.'

But 'thou dost but stand erect,' he says, and the interloper falls back foiled, while 'the nations cluster round,' and above them

> 'Thou, 'mid thy sheaves in peaceful seasons stored,
> Towerest supreme, victor without a blow,
> Smilingly leaning on thy undrawn sword.'

"This is the language, and these the feelings, of a man who has not taken up patriotism as a theme whereon he can conveniently and

EXTRACT FROM THE PREFACE

effectively descant, but whose habitual mood is one of proud thankfulness in belonging to a country where, if anywhere, he may feel

'The dignity of being alive.'

"Wordsworth has told us how,

'Among the many movements of his mind,

there were times at which he felt for England 'as a lover or a child.' It is as a lover that Mr. Austin habitually regards her, and if to a lover's fervour he unites somewhat of a lover's unconsciousness of any blemish in the worshipped face or form, such partiality is a thing we should be loth to exchange for any spirit of more coolly critical appraisement. Readers familiar with his whole contribution to poetry do not, however, need to be told that such emotion of heart in the presence of this ideal mistress is with him, as with Wordsworth, but one of 'many movements' which in their entirety represent a wide circuit of thought and feeling. In *The Human Tragedy* alone the complexity of elements is such as would have begotten in the work of an inferior artist an inevitable obscurity of design or incoherence of detail. Yet that poem assimilates easily into its narrative fabric such multifarious material as the collision of faith and reason; the conflict between human love and transcendental passion in a soul dedicated to heavenly uses but drawn aside for a time by an earthly emotion; the secret of the subtle spell exercised by Catholicism upon a pure and radiant human spirit which knows Doubt but as a shadow and Sin as a rumour; the immense, tragic irony of chance, as seen in the bewildered crossing and fortuitous overlapping of human lives, with all their momentous mutual interaction; the passionate abnegation or splendid immolation of self in the service of a great public cause; the heroic spectacle of a people that have long lain 'pillowed on their past' rising at the sudden summons of an idea to incarnate their dream of unity and freedom; the clash of theories, the dissonance of parties, the shock of hosts on the field ;—such are some of the constituents of a poem, the monumental scale of which, and the variety of its component parts, are not more remarkable than the artistic fusion of so large a mass of material as its argument comprehends."

MACMILLAN AND CO., LONDON.

[Turn over.

Now Ready. With Fourteen Illustrations. Fifth Thousand.

Extra Crown 8vo. Price 9s.

THE GARDEN THAT I LOVE

BY

ALFRED AUSTIN

TIMES—"It is a description in lucid and graceful prose of an old-fashioned garden and its cultivation, interspersed with genial colloquies between its owners and their guests, and enriched with occasional verse. Mr. Austin, who is greatly to be envied the possession of this delightful garden, and not less to be congratulated on his sympathetic appreciation of its charms, has rarely been so happily inspired. . . . Some of his admirers will wish for more of Mr. Austin's verse; for ourselves we are content with a volume which, though not in verse, is unmistakably the work of a poet."

SPECTATOR.—"We are glad to welcome Mr. Alfred Austin's delightful *Garden that I Love* in a compact book form. Mr. Austin is the laureate of gardens; he is, as Addison says, 'In love with a country life, where Nature appears in the greatest perfection, and furnishes out all those scenes that are most apt to delight the imagination.' In the preface to Mr. Austin's *English Lyrics*, Mr. William Watson writes: 'A nobly filial love of country, and a tenderly passionate *love of the country*—these appear to me the two dominant notes of this volume'; and in the new volume that has just appeared, the same dominant notes recur again and again. In his poems, Mr. Austin has described Spring's youthful face, where sunny smiles chase away the fleeting tears; Summer's serene rose-tinted beauty; the matured brilliance of Autumn; and the withered homeliness of Winter; and now he takes his readers behind the scenes, as it were, and shows them an ideal country-house with its heavy mullioned windows looking towards the morning and noontide sun, and its gabled front almost smothered in climbing roses and creepers. . . . *The Garden that I Love* is sure of a large and appreciative audience."

SATURDAY REVIEW.—"In this sunshiny book with the Tennysonian title, Mr. Alfred Austin makes a charming addition to the literature of the English garden. Not wholly of the garden and of gardening is the poet's discourse, nor wholly descriptive of the gardener's aims, his hopes and fears and joys. In part it treats of the designer's projects and handiwork; and in part it is a poetic descant on the work not made of hands—the glories, the surprises, the magic of Nature, that reward the single-hearted love of the gardener with a prodigal show of delights, ever varied and ever new. From both points of view Mr. Austin's volume is delightful. . . . Some pleasing interludes of conversation occur, in which Lamia and Veronica intervene with the writer and the Poet, not in a panegyric of the garden, but in personal talk, generally of a light and sportive humour. The Poet, indeed, recites some charming lyrics, and in his observations on poets and poetry assumes a graver tone."

PRESS NOTICES

GUARDIAN.—"*The Garden that I Love*, by Alfred Austin (Macmillan), is the work of a poet, artist, and gardener, who, having had the great luck to meet with an ideal house, surrounded it with an ideal garden. How this house and garden formed a convenient meeting place for 'friends in council,' and what these friends said and did, till the garden that they loved became the garden in which they loved, and the happy termination of their labours and loves, is most pleasantly told by Mr. Austin."

ACADEMY.—"Scarcely has the reader got through half a dozen pages of this bright little book before he finds himself on terms of close friendship with the author. Mr. Austin takes you at once into his confidence—or at least he appears to do so : he tells you by what good fortune he chanced to light upon his rural retreat ; he lets you pry into the details of his domestic arrangements ; and then, taking you kindly by the hand, goes with you round the Garden that he Loves. Month after month, from April till October, he depicts his garden in varying phase ; but, whatever its aspect, he somehow contrives to make the reader a partner in the simple pleasure which it yields. It is true that one is never quite sure, when listening to a poet, how far his descriptions are a direct reflex of the concrete, and how far the creation of his own imaginings. But no matter : whether real or imaginary, Mr. Austin's descriptions of his garden are equally delightful. . . . The volume is one which will be heartily enjoyed by every cultured reader. He who opens its pages shall find enshrined in them many a sage apophthegm, many a sparkling bit of dialogue, and many a verse of tenderness and grace."

STANDARD.—"The freshness of the morning sunlight, the perfume of the flowers, the songs of the birds, the sense of tranquil leisure are in this volume side by side with the companionship of pleasant women and of books, an air of culture, a gay philosophy of life, a dash of old-fashioned gallantry, and the give and take of happy humour. . . . There is much else in the book over which we could gladly linger ; for neither the garden that was loved, nor the love that was returned in its privacy of shade, exhaust the charm of this wholesome, imaginative, and genial outlook on Nature and on life."

DAILY TELEGRAPH.—"Mr. Alfred Austin has produced in *The Garden that I Love* (Macmillan), a little book full of delightful prose interspersed with equally charming poetry, the whole radiant with wit and mirth and delicate fancy. . . . The scientific pomologist may be glad to know how the author protects his orchard from grubs, and the lover of dainty poetry will certainly thank him for such a gem as the verses beginning 'Had I a Garden.'"

PALL MALL GAZETTE.—"Mr. Austin is a good writer of prose as well as verse ; and though he cannot conceal that he is a man of sharp insistent sensibilities, taste and scholarship combine to keep them in due restraint when literature is the business in hand. And here his style fits the subject very well indeed ; for, writing of an unformal garden, his language is negligent of formal grace, spreading over his pages as his wandering old rose-vine spreads over his walls. And the book is not all garden. A certain Martha-like Veronica is introduced into it, and a sparkling Lamia, and an unnamed Poet, in whom Mr. Austin (he need not deny it) doubles his part. These friends talk together on affairs of life and art and song ; and very good talk it is. But best of all is a piece of verse, ' If Love could Last,' more sweetly musical than anything else that we can remember in Mr. Austin's poetical work."

ST. JAMES'S GAZETTE.—"Mr. Austin's good fortune has proved the exceeding good fortune of his readers ; for never surely was the sense of the blessed beneficence of a garden, its boon of peace and refreshment to the spirit, expounded with more winning charm, or with more delicate truth of sentiment, than in this intimate and tender discourse about the Garden that he Loves. In no kind of writing, perhaps, than in this is it easier to miss just that *nuance* of tone and treatment that makes the difference between literature and twaddle. In these pleasant pages that *nuance* is most delicately apprehended. They are written not in poetic prose, but in prose that is essentially the prose of a poet, with the feeling and fancy of the poet. There is just the right mingling of actual poetry, just so much as to make us long for more ; and the snatches of verse introduced are in themselves most exquisite—it may be that their charm is heightened by their setting, but one does

PRESS NOTICES

not remember verse of Mr. Austin's that has charmed one more. There is sentiment enough to give life to the garden lore, and enough garden lore to give character to the sentiment. . . . Mr. Austin has seldom given us anything better than this delightful book. It is certainly one not to be missed by any lover of Nature—or any lover of graceful and charming prose."

SPEAKER.—"*The Garden that I Love* is pure delight. The sense of what Milton termed 'retired leisure' is in the book, and with it the scent of the flowers and much quick appreciation of country sights and sounds. Even whilst we ramble along the shady walks, or stop to gossip with the gardener, we never feel that we are 'buried' in any hopeless sense in the country, or that the charm of books and human fellowship is far to seek."

OBSERVER.—"Two ladies of temperaments that differ vastly, the Poet, and the creator of the garden—these four are the *dramatis personæ* in *The Garden that I Love*, the dainty volume which Mr. Alfred Austin has provided for the delight of many a weary town dweller, whose imagination, mayhap, has done him the good service to picture him, if only for an hour, the dweller in just such a haven of old-world loveliness as is here depicted. 'Lamia,' the brilliant perverse, 'Veronica,' the Martha-like mistress of the house that sat within the garden, the 'Poet,' with his verses and his delicate wisdom, and the narrator himself—in all of these humans we are deeply interested, and their apt meditations and meanderings are exquisitely attuned to the varying moods of the garden; but it is the garden itself that we learn to love in turning over Mr. Austin's enchanting pages. . . . He has succeeded with rare skill in suggesting the atmosphere of perfect peace that hangs, like a golden mist, over gardens which some one loves; and there is no garden lover, be he rich or poor, who will not feel that in *The Garden that I Love*, Mr. Austin has interpreted much that he has ofttimes felt, but for which, perhaps, he could find no adequate expression in words."

LITERARY WORLD.—"The most fragrant and refreshing book that we have had the happiness to review for many a long month. . . . Those who never care to see their favourite poet taking to prose, or their cherished prose-writer dropping into poetry, will find some comfort in the fact that there are some beautiful verses in *The Garden that I Love*. . . . Reviewing often means finding fault, but in this case that would be impossible. *The Garden that I Love* is a book to be thankful for. It is beautiful. It goes very close to perfection."

SCOTSMAN.—"It is a new thing for Mr. Alfred Austin to favour his readers with prose; and, indeed, the prose of his book *The Garden that I Love* is such as can be appreciated only by those who love poetry. The human interest of the book—that which lies in its touches of character—is not the less strong because it is intermittent and impressionist. The work is delightfully written. It will please in an immoderate degree men who are addicted to gardening, but one does not need to have so much of the original Adam in one as all that to enjoy a book so healthy and of so refined a sentiment, for a bookish man who had spent his life in towns will be refreshed by it as well."

LIVERPOOL DAILY POST.—"Why it should be so one finds it impossible to say, but the fact remains that to write about a garden a man must be a gentleman. Mr. Alfred Austin is the happy possessor of the necessary qualities, and his new book entitled *The Garden that I Love* is as fresh as the evening breeze across the whitened orchard tops of spring, in these days when, in literature, whiffs from the gutter strike the senses more frequently than the scent of new-mown hay. . . . We recommend every one to read his most delightful book."

MACMILLAN AND CO.,
BEDFORD STREET, STRAND, LONDON, W.C.

*Now Ready. With Fourteen Illustrations. Fourth Thousand.
Extra Crown 8vo. Price 9s.*

IN VERONICA'S GARDEN

BY

ALFRED AUSTIN

TIMES.—"Although sequels and continuations are proverbially perilous undertakings, we have little doubt that Mr. Alfred Austin's readers will gladly renew the acquaintance with Veronica's delightful garden and its genial occupants which they made in *The Garden that I Love*. The scheme of the new volume is the same as that of its predecessor. The garden is richer and more luxuriant, and its owner's or creator's love for it is more intense, than ever, and the illustrations with which the volume is enriched will make Mr. Austin's readers more eager than ever to share his love for and delight in it. The 'friends in council' whose colloquies enliven the garden and give an air of cultured retirement to Mr. Austin's pages are also the same as before, though their relationships are somewhat different. Veronica is now the wife of the Poet, while the anonymous gardener and the winsome Lamia appear to revolve somewhat erratically around this domestic centre. In both cases Mr. Austin blends in very delightful fashion his love of flowers and of simple rural delights with his love of gentle thoughts and gracious converse."

GUARDIAN.—"Mr. Austin has done well to follow up *The Garden that I Love* by *In Veronica's Garden*. It is really a second volume of the same work, and not only presupposes that the reader has read the first by frequent references to it, but is written on exactly the same lines, with the same *dramatis personæ*, the same quiet humour, and the same mixture of gardening, poetry, and moralising that made *The Garden that I Love* such pleasant reading. In one respect only can we trace any difference: the garden is still the central point of the book, but there is less of gardening in it, and more of moralisings and short essays; still the moralisings come in very naturally, and the essays, though short, are always to the point. There is the same healthy tone in this second volume that there was in the first; the same love of the country in all its aspects."

PRESTON GUARDIAN.—"*In Veronica's Garden* has grown as did *The Garden that I Love*. They are as twin apples from one bough. The last-named was ripe first, being a little nearer the sun, and gave our palate its first sweet taste of a new fruit. But the second is in the same style. Page after page one is plunged into the country. One has not merely a skilful word-painting of remembered beauty, but shares the emotion from the sight of the new leaves on the sweeping boughs, the lush grass, or the first swallow. The joys of the country are set out for town-bred people. There are several charming poems in the volume. A delightful one describes, in over a score of verses, 'The Passing of Spring.' Another embodies the real Christmas spirit better than any I have read. There is an imperial ring about the lines which appeal to

<blockquote>
All of British blood,—
Whether they cling to Egbert's Throne,
Or, far beyond the Western flood,
Have reared a Sceptre of their own,
</blockquote>

that should bring tender thoughts of the Motherland from many a far-off shore. I do not need to say more about the book. Whoever loves a garden will love it."

DAILY TELEGRAPH.—"A dainty piece of work is Mr. Alfred Austin's little volume, called *In Veronica's Garden*, which may be described as a continuation of his charming description of an English manor-house and its inhabitants—*The Garden that I Love*. Here, again, we meet with the modern representatives of Lamia and Veronica, with the amateur gardener himself, and with the Poet who is always ready to "oblige" with verses of delicate workmanship, written to suit place or season. Indeed, one of the chief charms of the book is the deft, unobtrusive way in which Mr. Austin has contrived to mingle poetry with his prose, and to gratify both those who love an elegant prose style and those who admire the lyrics of the author of *The Human Tragedy*. There is one especially beautiful sonnet, called 'A Dream of England,' in which a dweller in Italy imagines himself to—

PRESS NOTICES

> Hear the home-music of your Kentish skies,
> And dream that I am drenched with English dew.

Equally delightful in its own way is the 'Passing of Spring.'"

STANDARD—"Those who wander with Mr. Alfred Austin 'in Veronica's Garden' will be glad to find that it is none other than the Garden that he Loves. Not only is the place the same, but the company remains unchanged. Veronica is here again with her grave imperiousness and sweet addiction to household cares, and the playful Lamia is by her side trembling in mock earnest at her nod. He who tells the tale—the Keeper, shall we call him? of the pleasaunce—has lost nothing of his meditative delight in the infinite mutations of its loveliness, and the Poet comes back from Italy full of apt Virgilian learning, and ready at every turn to burst into English song that has a classic grace and freshness of its own. How much is fancy and how much portraiture? Where does the writer put himself into his record, and where is he content, with dainty dramatic touch, to furnish side lights to the picture of sincere and enthusiastic feeling? These are questions we do not care to ask, even if we believed that we could give dogmatic answers. The mind must be singularly ill-attuned to the finer spirit of the workmanship, which worries itself with analysis of this sort. It is enough to accept the volume gratefully as a delightful blending of the results of delicate observation and subtle thought with humour both kindly and refined. The dignity and rhythmical melodiousness of the prose would tell us, if we did not know in other ways, that the writer of this volume is a poet."

SPEAKER—"Mr. Austin, in giving us this book, has essayed to do an exquisite thing twice, and though some who like to have enjoyed their sensation and be done with it, may grumble, others will thank him for this further instalment of quiet days and quiet ways. The charm of his subject lies upon the book, so that even the list of flower-names becomes fragrant. . . . A delightful book."

ST. JAMES'S BUDGET—"This delightful volume has the full and fresh charm of *The Garden that I Love.*"

NATIONAL REVIEW—"A delightful book, which will be cordially welcomed by those who enjoyed *The Garden that I Love.* It has no mission, settles no problems, and is content to be charming, simple, and pleasure-giving."

DAILY NEWS—"Mr. Alfred Austin in *Veronica's Garden* continues his praises of *The Garden that I Love.* Once more he celebrates the delights of that secluded spot, the high walls of which shut out the 'ephemeral fret, fume, and turmoil of to-day,' and enclose a thousand simple enchantments; once more in those shaded walks and radiant borders we meet the perverse and lovely Lamia, the solicitous Veronica, the Poet whose verse gives the kindling touch that draws us into closer amity with the life of nature. Again it is the lover and tender of the garden that is the narrator. White of Selborne was not more precise than is Mr. Austin in noting the advent and ways of the blossoms and birds, or in observing the wayward, laggard, or hurrying steps of the season. The friends converse on many themes, on art, on the philosophy of life; their banter is gay and genial, their gravity never deepens into gloom. The poet quotes much from his favourite Virgil, and sings in graceful lyrics of the simple things of nature, of love, of friendship. He is the same gentle Conservative and patriot; the old faiths, the old ways are dear to him,

> And every wildling bird and leaf
> That gladdens English lanes.

His verse has the sincerity and spontaneity the talk of the friends sometimes lacks; and the note rings true that tells

> I would live nestled near my kind,
> Deep in a garden garth,
> That they who loved my verse might find
> A pathway to my hearth.

The beautiful old manor house and the garden are charmingly represented in the illustrations by A. Kohl and O. Lacour."

BLACKWOOD'S MAGAZINE—"Before the winter has finally set in, and while still the trees are in all their glory, Mr. Austin leads us back in his delightful way into the Garden which we all love. . . . It is just the book to lie in the embrasure of the window looking out upon a garden full of tangled sweetness, where lilies have lifted their tall heads, and roses blown from the beginning of time."

MACMILLAN AND CO.,
BEDFORD STREET, STRAND, LONDON, W.C.

www.ingramcontent.com/pod-product-compliance
Lightning Source LLC
Chambersburg PA
CBHW020103170426
43199CB00009B/378